Joseph T. McCann, PsyD, JD

Threats in Schools
A Practical Guide for Managing Violence

Pre-publication REVIEWS, COMMENTARIES, EVALUATIONS . . .

"Dr. McCann has provided a concise and informative way to analyze, understand, and respond to threats. His resource guide should be standard reading for school administrators, counselors, and teachers."

Dr. Ronald D. Stephens
Executive Director,
National School Safety Center,
California

"As school violence continues to tear at the heartstrings of America, Dr. McCann provides an enlightening and encouraging journey of discovery and hope. Rather than a knee-jerk reaction to this menacing problem, this is a well researched, useful, and 'practical guide for managing violence.' The book provides clear insight into this most provocative problem. After almost three decades as an FBI agent, profiling criminals, assessing threats, and now providing workplace violence prevention and response services to schools and the private sector, I can name no other source as complete, exhaustive, or well researched as this book.

Addressing violence through Dr. McCann's paradigm provides readers with a new awareness of threat and risk assessment. He goes beyond traditional explanations, providing a 'must-read' book for mental health professionals, faculty and administrators, law enforcement, probation and parole officers, judges, parents, and virtually anyone involved with the youth in America's schools. Our children deserve a safe environment in which to learn. Finally, here is a book with answers to some difficult questions concerning threats and risk. This book should be a required text for every teacher in America."

James T. Reese, PhD, FAAETS
Board Certified
in School Crisis Response;
Diplomate, Society for Police
and Criminal Psychology;
James T. Reese and Associates,
Lake Ridge, VA

More pre-publication
REVIEWS, COMMENTARIES, EVALUATIONS . . .

"Highly publicized incidents of school violence in recent years have created a demand for knowledge and solutions to deal with this shocking dilemma. Who is the 'typical school shooter'? What is the profile? How can we identify dangerous students? Finally, how can we prevent these events from occurring?

Threats in Schools provides the most complete and comprehensive body of knowledge to date on the topic of school violence. Joseph T. McCann outlines a realistic plan to identify, assess, and evaluate potentially violent students and situations. More important, he offers guidance through logical steps toward management and prevention of these events. This book is an invaluable resource for municipal and school managers, law enforcement officials, parents, and all who are concerned with violence in our schools."

Col. Robert K. Ressler, MS
Director, Forensic Behavioral Services International, Virginia;
Author, *Crime Classification Manual* and *Whoever Fights Monsters*

"Dr. Joseph McCann has combined his background in the field of adolescent mental health issues with his knowledge of risk management and threat assessment to produce a relevant, timely volume. Dr. McCann applies established principles of risk analysis to the sensitive, highly emotional subject of school violence. The book should be of use to school administrators, guidance counselors, law enforcement personnel, and mental health professionals working with children and adolescents in the process of evaluating the potential for violence in young people exhibiting threatening behavior."

Ronnie B. Harmon, MA
Associate Director,
Bellevue Hospital Center
Forensic Psychiatry Clinic,
New York City Health and Hospitals Corporation

"Drawing upon the latest research and practice in threat assessment and risk management, Dr. McCann presents a concise, comprehensive, and eminently practical guide for educators, mental health professionals, law enforcement personnel, and others charged with preventing school violence. For those who want to understand and practice the state of the art in assessing and managing threats in schools, this is the book to read."

Charles Patrick Ewing, PhD, JD
Author, *Kids Who Kill;*
Forensic Psychologist;
Professor of Law,
State University of New York, Buffalo

The Haworth Press®
New York • London • Oxford

NOTES FOR PROFESSIONAL LIBRARIANS AND LIBRARY USERS

This is an original book title published by The Haworth Press, Inc. Unless otherwise noted in specific chapters with attribution, materials in this book have not been previously published elsewhere in any format or language.

CONSERVATION AND PRESERVATION NOTES

All books published by The Haworth Press, Inc. and its imprints are printed on certified pH neutral, acid free book grade paper. This paper meets the minimum requirements of American National Standard for Information Sciences-Permanence of Paper for Printed Material, ANSI Z39.48-1984.

Threats in Schools
A Practical Guide for Managing Violence

THE HAWORTH PRESS
Risk Management
Joseph McCann
Senior Editor

Threats in Schools: A Practical Guide for Managing Violence by Joseph T. McCann

Other titles of related interest:

Kids Who Commit Adult Crimes: Serious Criminality by Juvenile Offenders by R. Barri Flowers

Violence As Seen Through a Prism of Color edited by Letha A. (Lee) See

The Shaken Baby Syndrome: A Multidisciplinary Approach edited by Stephen Lazoritz and Vincent J. Palusci

Identifying Child Molesters: Preventing Child Sexual Abuse by Recognizing the Patterns of the Offenders by Carla van Dam

From Hate Crimes to Human Rights: A Tribute to Matthew Shepard edited by Mary E. Swigonski, Robin S. Mama, and Kelly Ward

Political Violence and the Palestinain Family: Implications for Mental Health and Well-Being by Vivian Khamis

Program Evaluation and Family Violence Research edited by Sally K. Ward and David Finkelhor

Risky Business: Managing Employee Violence in the Workplace by Lynne Falkin McClure

Threats in Schools
A Practical Guide for Managing Violence

Joseph T. McCann, PsyD, JD

The Haworth Press®
New York • London • Oxford

The Haworth Press, Inc., 10 Alice Street, Binghamton, NY 13904–1580

Cover design by Jennifer M. Gaska.

Library of Congress Cataloging-in-Publication Data

McCann, Joseph T.
Threats in schools : a practical guide for managing violence / Joseph T. McCann.
p. cm.
Includes bibligraphical references (p.) and index.
ISBN 0-7890-1295-2 (hc. : alk. paper)—ISBN 0-7890-1296-0 (soft : alk. paper)
1. School violence—United States—Prevention. 2. Conflict management—Study and teaching—United States. I. Title.

LB3013.3 .M35 2001
371.7'82'0973—dc21

00—69708

To Michele, Alexander, and Ava

ABOUT THE AUTHOR

Joseph T. McCann, PsyD, JD, is a clinical psychologist at United Health Services Hospitals in Binghamton, NY. He also serves as a private forensic psychological consultant in criminal and civil cases and is licensed as both a psychologist and an attorney. His clinical, research, and teaching interests include assessing and managing interpersonal violence, threat assessment, and personality disorders.

Dr. McCann is a Fellow of the American Psychological Association and the Society for Personality Assessment. In addition, he is the founding editor of the *Journal of Threat Assessment* and the author of several other professional books, including *Stalking in Children and Adolescents: The Primitive Bond* and *Malingering and Deception in Adolescents: Assessing Credibility in Clinical and Forensic Settings*.

CONTENTS

Preface

Over the past several years a number of highly publicized school shootings in the United States have captured everyone's attention. These tragedies provoke questions among parents and within the community about the safety of children in schools, where it was once presumed that children were safe from serious harm. However, each new incident raises new concerns about the safety of schools.

As a clinical and forensic psychologist, I have had the opportunity to evaluate a considerable number of adolescents who have been referred for psychological evaluation due to aggressive or violent behavior. These evaluations have been conducted in both mental health and criminal justice settings, where there are often concerns about placement, amenability to treatment, risk of harm to others, learning disabilities, and serious mental disturbances that require treatment. In addition, I have conducted dozens of workshops over the past several years on a variety of topics, including forensic mental health issues and personality assessment. Whenever these workshops have been presented to those who work with children and adolescents in school settings or young offenders in the criminal justice system, questions have been raised about how to evaluate the potential for violence in students who have made threats in school settings.

The idea for this book arose out of my discussions with other professionals who evaluate the psychological status and mental health needs of children and adolescents in schools, mental health clinics, hospitals, residential treatment centers, correctional facilities, and private practice settings. In these discussions, I observed a pressing need among professionals for practical information on how to effectively assess and manage the threatening student. As such, this book is intended to serve as a concise guide to conceptualizing threats, assessing the violence potential in those students who have either made or who pose a threat of violence, and managing potentially violent situations in schools. Although the guidelines offered are based on empirical research, the focus is primarily on practical issues and recommendations for professionals who work with students in elementary and secondary school settings. Therefore, this guide can be used by teachers, psychologists, psychiatrists, school administrators, social workers, probation officers, guidance counselors, therapists, and other professionals who work either regularly or occasionally with children and adolescents. Parents may even find guidance to help them deal with situations involving their child as either a potential victim or perpetrator of violence.

The focus of this book is on students who make or pose a threat in school settings. Therefore, youth violence that is perpetrated in the community, family, or other settings is not discussed except to the extent that it relates to the threat of violence in schools. In addition, threatening situations involving adults in the school are not addressed, as these are construed primarily as an issue of workplace violence. However, student threats or violent behaviors that target a teacher or other staff member are discussed, since these situations center on how to deal effectively with the offending students.

Although much of the information provided here has an empirical basis, a detailed discussion of research has been avoided in favor of keeping the material concise and accessible to the practicing professional. Moreover, case examples are used in certain sections to illustrate points that are being made or to outline how suggestions apply in actual cases. Some case examples are taken from published accounts and are in the public domain; thus, no effort has been taken to alter identifying information. Other case examples have been taken from my professional work where I have either directly evaluated or been asked to consult in situations where students have either made or posed a threat to others. I have not provided any identifying information and I have altered slightly the facts for some of these cases to protect the anonymity of those involved. However, the basic dynamics and issues have been preserved.

It is my hope that this guide will offer direction to those who face the challenging task of dealing with student threats. Moreover, my hope is that as our knowledge of the causes of youth violence expands and more effective methods for coping with school violence emerge, we will continue to find reasonable solutions to this complex problem that are in the best interest of all students, the school, and community.

Joseph T. McCann

Acknowledgments

Several people deserve thanks for their support and assistance in the completion of this project. I would like to thank Martha Mason and Cheryl Slocum for their library support services. They have been of great help in tracking down research articles and materials that I have needed in my research. In addition, I would like to thank Faye Utyro and Dr. Leslie Major at United Health Services Hospitals for their support of my research and clinical work.

Several colleagues have been a source of great assistance to me over the years. In particular, I would like to extend a special note of thanks to Frank Dyer, Charles Patrick Ewing, Steve Lisman, Steve Lynn, J. Reid Meloy, and Ted Millon. In my work with young offenders, I have received valuable input from Ruben Reyes, Marshall Kuhns, Lee Wynn, Gary Cohen, Pam Vredenburgh, Linda Huntley, Connie Kinch, Jennifer Berryman, Alan Hochberg, Jay Flens, M. George Feeney, James F. Suess, Robert Tringone, Paul Retzlaff, June Schroeder, Charles Stephan, Eileen Cornell, Mary Miller, and Claudia Soriano.

I would also like to thank Bill Palmer and Rebecca Browne at The Haworth Press for their support of this project.

Finally, I would like to thank my family for all of their help and encouragement. My wife, Michele, continues to be a loving source of emotional and intellectual support that seems to know no limits. In addition, my son, Alexander, and daughter, Ava, have reaffirmed my love for learning, are an endless source of joy, and provided the basic motivation for writing this book. To my family I am eternally grateful.

Chapter 1

The Nature of Violence and Threat Assessment

Over the past several years, concern over the safety of students in schools has increased. Much of this concern stems from media reports of several school shootings. From 1996 to 1999, highly publicized school-based shootings took place in Jonesboro, Arkansas; Littleton, Colorado; Moses Lake, Washington; Conyers, Georgia; West Paducah, Kentucky; Pearl, Mississippi; Springfield, Oregon; Edinboro, Pennsylvania; and Fayetteville, Tennessee (Task Force on School Violence, 1999). According to the Task Force on School Violence (1999) in New York State, twenty-five students and four teachers were killed and another seventy-two students and three school employees were wounded in these shootings. As a result, considerable debate has been given to the causes of school-based violence and the steps that should be taken to reduce such violence, improve school safety, and maintain security in educational settings.

School shootings are not confined solely to middle and high schools. In the early part of 2000, a six-year-old boy in Michigan found a semiautomatic weapon in the house where he had been living with his mother and uncle. The house had been known to local authorities as a place where guns were often traded for crack cocaine. One day after a reported scuffle on the playground, the boy brought the gun to school and fatally shot a first-grade classmate. This tragedy illustrates that violence in schools is a social problem that spans all ages and grade levels.

These events have generated considerable concern among politicians, law enforcement personnel, mental health professionals, the general public, and school officials. Although the problem is multifaceted and a clear understanding of the causes and precipitants of school violence is complicated by the vast number of factors that must be considered, a pressing need exists to address this issue in light of a recent increase in multiple-victim, highly lethal shootings.

To illustrate the complexity of the problem, it may be useful to examine some of the more highly publicized school shootings that have occurred in recent years. Verlinden, Hersen, and Thomas (2000) examined several key groups of variables that were associated with these incidents, including individual, family, school/peer, social, situational, and attack-related behavioral factors for nine cases of multiple victim shootings in the three years prior to their study. Most major incidents were included in their sample, including Moses Lake, Washington (Barry Loukaitis); Bethel, Alaska (Evan Ramsey); Pearl, Mississippi (Luke Woodham); West Paducah, Kentucky (Michael Carneal); Jonesboro, Arkansas (Mitchell Johnson and Andrew Golden); Edinboro, Pennyslvania (Andrew Wurst); Springfield, Oregon (Kip Kinkel); Littleton, Colorado (Eric Harris and Dylan Klebold); and Conyers, Georgia (Thomas Solomon).

According to a detailed analysis of these cases, Verlinden and her colleagues found that most of the offending youths had a history of emotional disturbance, including depression and anger, a history of aggression, and previous threats of violence. Over half of the youths had generated drawings or writings that had violent themes; moreover, suicidal threats or ideation were very common among school assailants, while impulsivity was not. The attacks were carefully planned. Most of the youths either lacked parental supervision or had families in which there was considerable disruption, including a lack of support and a history of abuse or neglect. Moreover, many of the youths were socially isolated, rejected by peers, and had poor social skills. They often associated with peers who had conduct problems. In all of the cases, the youths had easy access to a gun, and most were fascinated with firearms and explosives. Many had extensive interest in video games, music, and other media that involved graphic violence. Furthermore, some of the youths showed evidence of deterioration in their functioning just prior to the attacks. Particularly notable was the fact that all of the youths clearly communicated their violent intentions to others and some even foretold the time and place the attacks would occur.

These findings illustrate that school violence is a problem that encompasses psychological, environmental, family, and situational factors; simple causal explanations are not possible. Furthermore, research into the dynamics of these cases is extremely useful because it expands our understanding of the unique factors that are associated with school violence and informs our efforts at prevention. There are different and sometimes conflicting approaches to applying research on school violence, however. One approach to using this applied research is to formulate "warning signs" of violence or profiles of the potentially lethal student, with the typical goal being removal of the student from school. Another approach may be to respond to threatening behavior in a manner that minimizes the potential for harm to others.

This guide is intended to be used by professionals who are in a position to evaluate and manage threatening behavior by students in school settings. It is intended to provide an approach to managing potentially violent situations in a manner that is interdisciplinary, preventive, and based on psychological concepts and principles. In this chapter, the prevalence of school violence will be examined and various approaches that have been set forth for dealing with the problem will be discussed. In addition, a critical analysis of many popular policies that are limited in their ability to prevent violence will be provided. Finally, an approach to evaluating and managing threatening behavior in school settings will be outlined, one that is based on a model of threat assessment and management whereby specific behaviors are targeted and a comprehensive evaluation and management plan is developed. The remainder of this guide will specify this approach in greater detail, including a discussion of various types of threats, how they are communicated, risk factors associated with violent behavior, ways to assess and manage threats, and special situations where potential for violence exists.

VIOLENCE IN SCHOOLS

Although violence among young people is a serious concern in society, one of the primary concerns in recent years has been the safety of children when they are at school. Between 1992 and 1994, seventy-six students were murdered or committed suicide while in school, according to data collected by the National Center for Education Statistics (Kaufman et al., 1998). During the 1996-1997 school year, 10 percent of public schools had at least one incident of serious violence that resulted in a report being made to the local police or law enforcement agency. Despite public concern over safety in schools, data show that if a student is the victim of violence, it is more likely to occur away from school rather than while the student is on school grounds. According to the National Center for Education Statistics, in 1996, 255,000 students between the ages of twelve and eighteen were the victims of some nonfatal violent crime (e.g., rape, assault) and 671,000 students were victims in violent incidents that occurred off school grounds. Moreover, most murders and suicides involving children and adolescents occurred while the victims were not at school.

Although these statistics support the notion that more violent incidents involving children and adolescents occur away from school than at school, violent incidents in school settings continue to cause alarm regarding the safety of students. Schools are generally viewed as places where children should be safe and secure to facilitate their learning and growth. The fact that a young person is more likely to be the victim of violence away from school does not automatically lead to assurances that students will be safe at school. Between 1989 and 1995, for example, the number of students who feared being attacked or harmed at school rose from 5 percent to 9 percent, which represents an increase of about 2.1 million students over this six-year period (Kaufman et al., 1998).

According to research by Verlinden, Hersen, and Thomas (2000), the number of violent deaths in school settings since the 1992-1993 academic year has steadily decreased. However, violent incidents involving multiple victims has increased. Between 1992 and 1995, there was an average of one violent school-based incident involving multiple victims each year, whereas between 1995 and 1999 there was an average of five such incidents per year. Therefore, while school violence may be declining in some respects, more highly publicized lethal incidents involving several victims may be contributing to increased concerns about school safety.

APPROACHES TO COMBATING SCHOOL VIOLENCE

Many policies and programs have been proposed or implemented around the United States to deal with the problem of violence in the schools. Among the more visible and popular attempts are the use of metal detectors at entrances, banning bookbags, stationing police officers or security guards at school entrances, and installing video monitors and other security equipment. Another highly publicized change has been implementation of "zero tolerance" policies for managing school violence in which any behavior, threat, or gesture that is remotely indicative of potential violence results in the student being immediately suspended or expelled from school. In some instances, the use of zero tolerance policies has resulted in questionable responses to supposed threats as some students, who write poems or short stories with violent themes and submit them as part of a formal school assignment, are identified as a threat and suspended from school.

Other approaches to dealing with school violence include the passage of legislation that seeks to increase punishment for those who commit acts that pose a risk to others. For example, some states have passed laws calling for mandatory incarceration for one year or more if a student brings a gun onto school grounds. In other instances, legislation has been proposed to make parents criminally liable for the actions of their children. Many of these legal mandates seek to set up strong deterrents that are believed to reduce the risk for future school violence.

Several problems exist with many of the approaches that have been either implemented or proposed for dealing with school violence. For example, zero tolerance policies are essentially unproven with respect to their ability to prevent violence because they fail to target situations where a student does not make a threat, or threats are not known to school officials, and the student later commits an act of violence. In other circumstances, laws that make parents criminally liable for the acts of their children impose a punishment "after the fact," where violence has already occurred. Clearly, the most desirable approach to threatening behavior and violence in schools is to prevent harm before it occurs.

Another popular approach to addressing the problem of school violence is heightening awareness of the "warning signs" of violence. In particular, printed material and published literature is often circulated to sensitize parents, teachers, school administrators, and others to the emotional and behavioral indicators that suggest a specific student may represent a heightened risk for becoming violent. This particular approach raises serious questions about the problem of erroneous or inaccurate judgments being made about some students.

The prediction of violent behavior based on a specific indicator that is believed to be associated with violence, namely a clear threat, can be conceptualized according to a basic contingency table as outlined in Figure 1.1. This grid is similar to others that have been utilized in the field of violence prediction (Quinsey et al., 1998). When the presence or absence of a student threat is used to make a decision on an appropriate course of action, four possible outcomes can occur. The student who makes an overt threat and ends up committing a violent act is represented by the upper left quadrant in which there has been an accurate prediction of violence based on the threat. However, if the student makes an overt threat but has no intention of carrying out the threat and does not end up becoming violent, then a false alarm error has occurred in which a prediction was made that a nonviolent student will become violent. This situation is represented by the upper right quadrant of Figure 1.1 and illustrates that someone who makes an overt threat may not necessarily pose a threat of violence (Fein, Vossekuil, and Holden, 1995).

Two other outcomes are possible if a student does not make an overt threat. The lower left quadrant represents a situation in which the student does not make an overt threat but commits an act of violence. This judgment involves relying on the absence of a threat to make the determination that a student will not be violent. In some cases, however, the student may conceal his or her intention of doing something violent, but may exhibit other indicators of violence potential that are missed if reliance is placed solely on the presence or absence of an overt threat. This situation results in an erroneous prediction of nonviolence, which highlights the notion that someone who poses a real threat of violence may not necessarily make a threat (Fein, Vossekuil, and Holden, 1995). Finally, the lower right quadrant

FIGURE 1.1. Decision Accuracy for Predicting Student Violence

		Predicted Outcome	
		Violent Behavior	**No Violent Behavior**
Predictor	**Student Threat**	Accurate Prediction of Student Violence	Erroneous Prediction of Student Violence
	No Student Threat	Erroneous Prediction of Student Non-Violence	Accurate Prediction of Student Non-Violence

of Figure 1.1 represents an accurate prediction of nonviolence based on the absence of an explicit threat.

This model of predictive decision making reflects many of the problems that are inherent when relying on any single predictor of violence, such as when a threat is relied upon to make a judgment about future violence. If this model is applied to zero tolerance policies, for example, a threat made by a student, even if done jokingly or without any intent or means for carrying it out, would result in the expulsion of the student based on the notion that all students who threaten are considered potentially violent. As a result, two types of errors will be made under threat management strategies in schools that adopt zero tolerance policies. Some students who threaten yet never act violently will be incorrectly viewed as violent. Likewise, students who do not threaten yet later become violent constitute an erroneous prediction of nonviolence and are not identified under zero tolerance policies. Moreover, it is likely that schools with a zero tolerance stance do so to demonstrate to school boards, the public, and governmental agencies that they have a method for dealing with school violence. However, such policies are prone to error if the complex relationship between threats and violence is not recognized.

Many of the policies and procedures that have been implemented for dealing with school violence, such as zero tolerance or enforcing stricter criminal penalties for youngsters who bring a weapon to school, arise out of a need to respond to the risk of violence in schools. These policies create an appearance of reasonable and well-intended responses that may provide some reassurance to students, their parents, and the community. However, they can be faulted for several reasons, including the fact that they have not been tested empirically, intervene after the fact, or result in critical errors when identifying those students who actually pose a threat to others.

One approach to managing school violence that holds considerable promise for dealing with threatening behavior among students is the threat assessment model developed by the United States Secret Service. This model is based on an approach to preventing targeted violence that conceptualizes threatening behavior and violence differently than do traditional models of violence prediction. Although this model was developed in large part by evaluating and studying incidents involving threats to individuals falling under the protective mandate of the United States Secret Service, it is preventive in nature and also can be adopted to evaluate and manage threatening behavior in school settings.

UNDERSTANDING THREAT ASSESSMENT AND MANAGEMENT

Threat assessment has been defined by Fein and Vossekuil (1998) as "the process of gathering and assessing information about persons who may have the interest, motive, intention, and capability of mounting attacks against public officials and figures" (p. 7). Similarly, the management of threats has also been referred to as "protective intelligence" and is defined as having the goal of preventing an attack on the identified target. Although these definitions and principles arose within the law enforcement community in which the goal has been to assess and manage threats toward public figures, they can be readily applied to the problem of school-based threats and violence.

According to Fein and Vossekuil (1998), there are three components to a protective intelligence program. The first involves identifying various ways in which an individual may present a risk for attack or violence. In some cases, this may involve an overt statement made verbally, in writing, through electronic mail, or by some other means. Moreover, the threat may be direct, indirect, or conditional. If one applies the identification process to school settings, an example of a direct threat would be when a male student tells a female teacher that he is going to attack her physically when she walks to her car after school is let out for the day. An indirect threat might involve the student saying something aloud to a peer, knowing that the teacher can hear: "Teachers at this school better watch their backs when they leave at night." A conditional threat might occur when the student hands in a paper and says, "If I don't pass this, I'm going to mess you up." Not only is the type of threat important, but so is the manner in which it is made known to the victim, other students, and school administrators. The manner in which threats are brought to the attention of others will determine how they are handled by school officials.

The second component of a protective intelligence program is assessment and evaluation of the threat (Fein and Vossekuil, 1998). Information must be gathered about the person making the threat, including situational or conditional factors that impact the ability of the person to carry out the threat. More specifically, it is important to answer such questions as whether the threatener has a specific plan, access to weapons, conditions under which the threat will be carried out, and so forth. An assessment of the person making the threat, including various factors that may increase or reduce his or her potential for violence, must also be considered. Other components of the data-gathering phase include an appraisal of the type of information that has been obtained from various sources, including the reliability and credibility of informants or witnesses, people to whom the threat has been communicated, and peer reactions to any threatening statements. In the school setting, assessment and evaluation of data sources would include an evaluation of whether a communicated threat is considered to be gossip among students, a student trying to get another student into trouble, and similar appraisals of credibility.

The third major component of a protective intelligence program is case management (Fein and Vossekuil, 1998). After enough information has been obtained to make a determination as to whether the identified person poses a threat of violence, a plan is implemented in cases where evidence points to presence of a risk. In such situations, a protective intelligence model constitutes a better response to threats in school settings than do broad policies such as zero tolerance, in which a student is immediately expelled for making a threat (regardless of how vague the threat is or of the person's intent) or approaches are implemented after the fact. A threat management program calls for a plan to be developed whereby a series of graded steps can be taken. The severity of the threat can be evaluated and a continuum of interventions are available. Among the least restrictive and intrusive measures would be monitoring the identified student, group of students, or situation. Intermediate steps might include referral of the student for psychological assessment and treatment, temporary removal of the student from the school or classroom, and a series of scheduled contacts with specific individuals (e.g., hourly checking in with an assistant principal; weekly meetings with family members). More restrictive intervention strategies would include expulsion of the student, referral of the case to law enforcement officials where a criminal act has been committed, and involuntary hospitalization if the student poses an imminent threat of suicide or harm to others.

The application of threat assessment and management programs in schools is possible without incurring large monetary costs. A direct and inexpensive way of implementing such a program would be to assemble a threat evaluation and management team that is interdisciplinary and comprised of staff within the school system who are trained in the identification, assessment, and management of threatening behavior by students (Mohandie, 2000). Fein and Vossekuil (1998) offer several questions that organizations can utilize when developing and implementing a threat assessment and management program. Their questions, which have been reformulated and applied to school settings, can be asked by school administrators prior to undertaking such a program:

1. How does the school currently define its responsibilities to assess and manage school violence?
2. Does the school district currently have responsibilities to manage school violence? Will responsibilities be imposed upon the school in the future?
3. What approaches and policies does the school currently use to manage school violence?
4. What legal responsibilities exist for protecting students?
5. How often does a violent or threatening situation arise in the school?
6. What currently happens when a student, teacher, or some other person makes a threat in school?
7. What should happen when a threat or report of a threat is received?
8. Do other concerns arise in the school, such as stalking, sexual harassment, bullying, and other forms of harassment?

Fein and Vossekuil (1998) noted that once these questions have been fully explored and the organization determines that a threat assessment and management program is appropriate, a number of other questions must be answered. Once again, reformulating their questions so that school districts can perform a self-study, these questions are as follows:

1. Which staff members and which professionals will make up the threat assessment and management team?
2. How will the team maintain and share information and expertise it gathers over time?

3. How will new members of the team be oriented to the procedures of assessing and managing school threats?
4. How much emphasis and balance will be given to the following issues: school administration, mental health, education, legal, and law enforcement?
5. To whom will the team report (e.g., school board, school administration, families)?
6. Does a mechanism exist for the team to learn from its experiences and thus improve efforts at assessing and managing threats?
7. How will case information be stored and retrieved for use?

Many of the answers to these questions, including whether a process for assessing and managing threats is possible in the school, will depend on a number of considerations. For instance, it may or may not be feasible to develop a formal program; in some cases, these procedures may need to be implemented with existing staffing patterns. However, any threat assessment and management program that is developed for school settings should be interdisciplinary in nature and include a school administrator, mental health professional, guidance counselor or school social worker, and teacher who is familiar with the students. The issue of whether to have input from law enforcement is a sensitive one because of concerns about criminal charges being filed, confidentiality when sharing information about a student with someone who is not employed by the school district, and so forth. It may be necessary to have a law enforcement officer available for consultation as needed, where student information can be presented anonymously, with more active involvement if the situation requires reporting a criminal act. If schools have a security officer or administrator in charge of security issues, this person would serve as a favorable alternative to outside law enforcement officers and could also assist in cases where a referral to law enforcement is necessary.

CONCLUSION

The problem of school violence has come to the forefront of national attention due to several highly publicized school shootings in which there were multiple victims. Although most violence perpetrated against children and adolescents occurs outside of school settings, a need remains for managing potentially violent situations in schools to ensure that students can learn in a safe and secure environment. Although several policies and interventions have been proposed or implemented to combat the problem of school violence, many are based on a retroactive approach in which changes are made after violence has occurred or a simplistic view of threatening and violent behavior. An effective approach for dealing with threatening and violent behavior in schools is one based on a protective intelligence model in which an individual student, group of students, or situation is identified as posing a potential threat of violence or harm to others. Threats are then evaluated through the comprehensive collection of data, including an assessment of several factors, such as psychological, social, familial, situational, and legal variables. Once an evaluation of the threat has been made and case management is required, a variety of interventions may be considered depending on the specific needs of the situation.

In the remainder of this guide, each of these three steps to evaluating and managing threats (i.e., identification, assessment, and management) will be discussed. Chapter 2 deals with defining various types of threats, the ways in which they can be communicated, and behaviors that may lead to violence and aggression toward others. In Chapters 3 and 4, assessment of violent and threatening behavior will be discussed. Chapter 5 outlines general procedures for managing violence, and Chapter 6 deals with special situations (e.g., arson, sexual violence) that require unique considerations.

Chapter 2

Types of Threats and Violence

The pressing need to deal with threatening and violent behavior is being felt in all schools, regardless of grade level or geographic location. However, considerable risk exists of misguided or ineffective programs being implemented if policies or interventions are set forth without a clear definition of what is meant by violent or threatening behavior or a clear understanding of these problems. One recent incident in New Jersey illustrates many of the difficulties and controversies that can arise from attempts to deal with threatening student behavior that are based on unclear definitions or a failure to take various factors such as context and motive into account ("Kindergartners Suspended," 2000). Four six-year-old boys were reportedly pointing their fingers and pretending to shoot one another in a game of "cops and robbers." They were suspended by the principal for three days as a disciplinary action because several other students were apparently "visibly upset" by the actions of the four boys, which were viewed as "serious threats." Although the school district has been criticized, the superintendent supported the principal's response because recent school shootings dictated that the school take a "conservative view" toward violence in an effort to prevent future incidents.

While school administrators must take actions to keep students safe and school settings secure, considerable room remains for overreaction and taking actions that fail to properly distinguish genuine threats from behaviors that do not present a realistic risk of violence. As noted earlier, a difference exists between students who make a threat and those who pose a threat. Furthermore, policies and interventions that focus on clear and overt threats provide a false sense of security because some students who become violent do not make any overt threat. In addition, some behaviors that are construed as threatening, such as those in the previously described case, may not actually constitute a threat based on the context in which they occur. Although permitting six-year-old children to play a game involving the simulated use of guns may not be appropriate for some settings, these actions would hardly constitute threats against other students, let alone "serious threats."

Therefore, an appropriate starting point for identifying and assessing threatening and violent behavior is to define specific terms and concepts. In this chapter, the terms *aggression, violence,* and *threats* will be defined, including various subtypes of each behavior. Several factors can be used to further differentiate types of aggressive and violent behaviors, including how they are expressed, the person toward whom they are directed, and the perpetrator's actual intent. In addition, different types of threats will be identified based on how they are made, the clarity with which they are made, and the threatener's intent. In this way, accurate assessments and more effective interventions and case management strategies are possible.

WHAT IS AGGRESSION?

The definition of aggression has been approached from psychoanalytical, behavioral, neurobiological, and social psychological perspectives. An operational definition was offered by Buss (1961), who defined aggression as "a response that delivers noxious stimuli to another organism" (p. 1). Although this broad definition can be applied to animals as well as humans, Geen (1998) offered a social psychological definition that views aggression as a group of behaviors that are functionally different from one another and yet have as their goal the harming of another person. One of the practical features of social psychological definitions is that they lend themselves readily to the conceptualization and formulation of threatening behavior in school settings.

Bushman and Anderson (1998) noted that aggression has typically been measured by social psychologists according to a number of dimensions. These include whether the aggressor actually intends to harm the victim, has an expectation that the aggressive act will have its intended effect, and expresses aggression physically or verbally. Therefore, measurement of aggression in laboratory settings has been possible by attending to such factors as the intent and expectations of the aggressor. As a result, the behavioral classification of aggression has been split into such categories as direct physical aggression (e.g., hitting), indirect physical aggression (e.g., stealing someone's belongings), direct verbal aggression (e.g., insult), and indirect verbal aggression (e.g., provocative statements).

This social psychological paradigm lends itself to the practical conceptualization of threatening statements because it highlights the importance of considering several dimensions of a threat. For instance, whether or not the threatener intends to carry out the threat, a specific victim has been identified, the threatener wishes to be believed, and the threat is explicitly made are all variables that should be considered when evaluating the nature of a student threat.

Another important distinction that social psychologists make among aggressive actions has to do with the motivations of the aggressor and the underlying reasons he or she acts aggressively toward the victim. Two types of aggression have been distinguished based on underlying motivation: *instrumental* and *affective*. Instrumental aggression is motivated primarily by a need or desire to obtain some identifiable goal (Geen, 1998; Huesmann, 1998). It is motivated by an expectation or belief that the aggressive behavior will result in the person getting what he or she wants. An example of instrumental aggression would be a student who targets a smaller student and uses verbal and physical intimidation to get the smaller student's lunch money. In this example, the aggression is directed at the identifiable goal of obtaining money. Huesmann (1998) noted that instrumental aggression depends largely on the aggressor having a large number of organized aggressive behaviors that are relied upon for solving problems, as well as a belief that aggression is an appropriate and acceptable way to act in various situations.

Affective aggression is motivated solely by an intent to harm or injure the victim (Geen, 1998; Huesmann, 1998). This form of aggression is associated with intense emotions such as anger, hostility, hate, or reactive aggression. An example would be a student who becomes increasingly more angry and erupts by pushing or hitting another student after being incessantly teased. In this case, the aggression is directed at stopping the teasing, but angry emotions result in a feeling of wanting to injure or harm the provocative student. Individuals who are prone to exhibit reactive aggression tend to have higher levels of emotional reactivity and are more likely to attribute hostile motives to other people in situations that provoke negative emotions (Huesmann, 1998). In addition, affective forms of aggression result when individuals who have a fragile or vulnerable self encounter a threat to their self-esteem or feelings of personal adequacy.

Another distinction has been made between *proactive* and *reactive* aggression (Smithmyer, Hubbard, and Simons, 2000). Proactive aggression is deliberate, goal-oriented, and occurs without provocation. Reactive aggression is in response to some perceived threat or provocation and is primarily defensive in nature. According to Smithmyer and her colleagues, proactive aggression is characterized by individuals who have an expectation that aggression will lead to a positive outcome. Similarly, instrumental aggression is characterized by youths who have positive feelings about their aggressive actions, suggesting a lack of remorse or empathy for victims (Cornell et al., 1996). Toward this end, assessment of violence potential in a student who is believed to pose a threat to others should address the student's attitudes and beliefs about aggression as a method for resolving conflict. A positive view of violent behavior, with the expectation of a favorable outcome and lack of empathy for victims, indicates a propensity for the student to engage in calculated, planned, and predatory acts of violence that are directed at obtaining some goal. Negative views of aggression as a form of conflict resolution indicate a propensity for emotional, reactive, or abrupt aggression that is directed toward the elimination of a perceived threat.

Understanding the motivations of an aggressor can help in the evaluation of potential threats. One factor to consider when evaluating the nature, severity, and seriousness of a threatening communication is whether the student intends to carry out the threat. That is, evaluations should consider what the student making the threat wishes to accomplish by making a threat or why he or she may have chosen not to make an overt threat prior to committing an act of violence. Before delineating these aspects of threat assessment, it is necessary to define what is meant by the term violence.

WHAT IS VIOLENCE?

The specific definition of violence one adopts depends largely on theoretical perspective. Using a neurobiological approach, Volavka (1995) defined violence as aggression that occurs among humans and differentiated it from animal behavior. From a law enforcement perspective, Fein, Vossekuil, and Holden (1995) defined violence as a process rather than a specific act or set of acts. In their monograph, *Threat Assessment: An Approach to Prevent Targeted Violence,* which was prepared for the National Institute of Justice of the United States Department of Justice, they noted that violent behavior does not occur in a vacuum. If one carefully considers all facets of violent acts, it becomes clear that they "often are the culmination of long-developing, identifiable trails of problems, conflicts, disputes, and failures" (p. 3).

Two types of violence that have been specified in research studies are *relational* and *predatory* (Ellickson and McGuigan, 2000). Relational violence refers to those acts that occur in the context of interpersonal disputes between family members, friends, or peers, while predatory violence refers to those acts that are directed toward obtaining some goal or material gain, such as mugging or robbery, and which are part of a larger pattern of criminal behavior. These two types of violence are similar to those outlined by Meloy (1988), who discussed some useful differences between affective and predatory violence. Affective violence is characterized by such things as a subjective experience of emotion, reactivity to a perceived threat, autonomic nervous system arousal, a time-limited behavioral sequence, lowered self-esteem, and behavior directed toward the elimination or reduction of a threat. Predatory violence is characterized by minimal or no autonomic nervous system arousal, no conscious experiencing of emotion, heightened self-esteem, no perceived threat, variable goals, and a higher level of cognitive planning. Consequently, the emotional display and reactivity to perceived threat in affective violence precede the violent act and make it more likely that a victim will foresee the aggression coming. On the other hand, absence of emotion and careful planning that accompany predatory violence increase the likelihood of a surprise attack and make the violence more difficult to predict.

Another way of specifying different types of violence is with respect to mode of expression (i.e., verbal versus physical) and target of the violence (e.g., self, other, inanimate object). For instance, Silver and Yudofsky (1991) developed a means of identifying aggressive or violent incidents in hospital settings according to mode of expression and type of victim: verbal aggression; physical aggression against the self; physical aggression against objects; and physical aggression against other people. These classifications are also useful for classifying specific types of violent behavior that a student may exhibit.

Table 2.1 outlines these classifications and provides examples of student behavior that represent each form of violence.

TYPES OF THREATS

The standard dictionary definition of threat is "an expression of intention to hurt, destroy, or punish" or "an indication of imminent danger, harm, evil, etc." (Guralnik, 1970, p. 1482). Meloy (1999) defined threat as "a written or oral communication that implicitly or explicitly states a wish or intent to damage, injure, or kill the target" (p. 90). These definitions convey several notable aspects of threatening behavior. More specifically, threats can be expressed or overt; they may also be made without a verbal statement by the person posing the threat. In other words, a threat may also be a gesture, an unstated risk, or a hidden intent to harm. The expression or indication of a threat may or may not be known to the potential victim.

In addition, threats can be distinguished by the manner in which they are communicated. Hinman and Cook (2001), in citing the work

TABLE 2.1. Types of Student Violence

I. Verbal Violence
- A. Swearing and foul language
- B. Insults, name-calling, and verbal provocation
- C. Verbal threats of violence (directly to the victim or indirectly through third parties)
- D. Suicidal threats or comments
- E. Written messages, threats, or communications

II. Physical Violence Toward Self
- A. Suicide gesture or attempt
- B. Self-mutilation or intentionally harming self
- C. Risk-taking behavior that results in injury to self

III. Physical Violence Toward Property or Objects
- A. Breaking furniture or objects
- B. Fire setting
- C. Slamming objects
- D. Vandalism

IV. Physical Violence Toward Others
- A. Threatening with a weapon
- B. Hitting, pushing, or physical assault
- C. Causing physical injury to another person
- D. Injuring with a weapon

of Calhoun (1998), noted that threats may be expressed through nonverbal behavior, not just verbal or written communications. They noted that inappropriate communications can be defined as any contact or approach behavior toward a potential victim that may involve activity that is in preparation for violence or behavior that evokes fear in the victim, such as the giving of bizarre gifts, nonverbal gestures, and planning activities. Consequently, it is possible to differentiate various types of threats according to whether they are overt or concealed, written or verbal, and so forth. Overt threats are those in which there is a clear expression of intent to commit some act that is likely to harm another person. Concealed threats, on the other hand, are those in which the person or persons posing the threat become a source of potential harm or danger, but this threat is not made known to the potential victim or to others who may be in a position to intervene. In addition, there are several dimensions to threats that must be considered, including the content of the threatening communication, the intent of the person making the threat, the victim's perception of the threat, how credible or believable the threat is, the motivation behind the threat, and secondary gain that may occur from making a threat.

Several types of threats can be differentiated in terms of motive, intent, and clarity of expression. As cited by Hinman and Cook (2001), Calhoun (1998) set forth three categories of threats against federal judges based on the extent of planning that has gone into carrying out the threat: *specious, enhanced,* and *violent* threats. Specious threats consist of communications that sound plausible, but further examination reveals no evidence of planning, intent, or effort to carry out the threat. A specious threat occurred in one case where a student telephoned a bomb threat into the school. He was apprehended, prosecuted for menacing, and sentenced to a juvenile detention facility. The evaluation revealed that he had no intention of acting on the threat, had not taken any actions to carry out the threat (e.g., searching for bomb recipes on the Internet), and had reportedly made the threat because he and some friends "wanted a day off" from school. Enhanced threats are those in which the threatener has engaged in some behavior to further the threat, although there is no evidence of imminent risk for violence or life-threatening circumstances. Violent threats are those in which some act of violence has been perpetrated along with the threat. A threat can be further categorized in terms of whether the threatener is capable of carrying it out (i.e., potent versus impotent), the clarity with which it is made (i.e., direct versus veiled), and the timing or conditions under which it may be carried out (i.e., immediate, conditional, deferred).

Meloy (1999) identified two different types of threats, namely *instrumental* and *expressive*. Instrumental threats are those in which the person intends to control or influence another person by using the threat as a negative consequence. An example of an instrumental threat would be a bully who says to another student, "You're going to have to walk home today. If you get on the bus after school, I'm going to mess you up bad." In this situation, the threatener's intent is to intimidate the other student and to influence his or her behavior. Expressive threats are motivated primarily by a need to regulate the emotions of the person making the threat. An example would be a student who, after being mercilessly teased by a group of peers, shouts, "I can't stand it anymore. You're dead." In this situation, the threat arises out of intense frustration and anger and is intended as a means of venting rage.

Given the various ways in which threats can be classified, it is important to consider the different dimensions about a threatening communication when conducting an assessment. Table 2.2 provides various types of threats along with their definitions, and Table 2.3 provides questions that evaluators can ask about a threatening communication to help develop a clear understanding of its nature. Many of these threats overlap one another and more than one descriptor can be used for a single threat. For example, a concealed/potent threat is one that is not communicated to others, yet the person posing the threat is fully capable of harming the intended victim.

In addition, Meloy (1999) noted that threats can be analyzed in terms of their content, which may reveal qualities about the psychological defenses and emotional state of the threatener. For instance, some threats involve devaluation in which the threatener attributes exaggerated negative qualities to the victim (e.g., "All jocks deserve to die"). Other threats involve projection, in which the person attributes unacceptable feelings, thoughts, or feelings about himself or herself (e.g., anger, homosexual impulses) to others (e.g., "Death to all gays because they always try to come on to you"). Other defenses include denial, in which the threatener denies ever having made a threat to avoid punishment or to reduce tension or conflict. Meloy noted that the specific content of the threat can be used to help those responsible

TABLE 2.2. Types of Threats

Type of Threat	Definition
Conditional	These are to be carried out only if some condition or set of circumstances occurs.
Concealed	There is an intent to harm someone, but the threat is not communicated to anyone else.
Delayed	These are to be carried out at some time in the future, such as a particular date or time or in a specific situation.
Direct/Overt	The threatener is clear with respect to his or her intended victim, intent, and/or motive.
Enhanced	Associated with some action or behavior that demonstrates an effort to carry out the threat.
Expressive	Motivated by the need to regulate and modulate emotions (e.g., anger, rage).
Immediate	Carried out immediately or are associated with an imminent threat.
Impotent	Person making the threat is incapable of carrying it out.
Instrumental	Motivated by the need to control or influence behavior of another person.
Potent	Person making the threat is capable of carrying it out.
Specious	Sounds real, but later turns out to be false alarm or associated with no effort to carry out threat.
Vague/Nonspecific	Type of harm and/or intended victim is not made clear.
Veiled	Vague or unclear with respect to threatener's intent in acting on the threat and/or motive.
Violent	Associated with some act of violence that is to be carried out.

for evaluating and managing threats understand a threatener's state of mind and determine the relative risks involved.

One way this can be done is by conceptualizing defense mechanisms according to their level of severity. The *Diagnostic and Statistical Manual of Mental Disorders*, Fourth Edition (DSM-IV) (American Psychiatric Association, 1994), presents a defensive functioning scale in which a level of severity is assigned to specific defense mechanisms, which are defined as "automatic psychological processes that protect the individual against anxiety and from the awareness of internal or external dangers or stressors" (p. 751). Therefore, defense mechanisms can be used to understand threats, which are often made out of fear, a perception of danger, or in response to some internal or external conflict. Furthermore, psychological defense mechanisms

TABLE 2.3. Dimensions to Assess When Evaluating Types of Threats

Dimension	Inquiry
Intent	Does the person intend to carry out the threat?
Victim	Has a specific, general, or any victim been identified?
Clarity	Has a clear threat been made or has it merely been suggested? Are there any conditions to the threat?
Believability	Does the threatener wish to be believed?
Motive	What does the threatener wish to accomplish? Is there any secondary gain?
Manner of Expression	How has the threat been communicated?
Context	In what context has the threat occurred?

are coping strategies that represent action-orientation (e.g., acting out, apathetic withdrawal, passive aggression), cognitive distortions (e.g., devaluation, idealization, autistic fantasy), inhibition (e.g., displacement, intellectualization), or the disavowing of certain thoughts, feelings, or impulses (e.g., denial, projection).

The content of a threatening communication is key data that provide insight into the threatener and his or her propensity for acting violently. More specifically, a threat can communicate conditions under which the threat will be carried out (e.g., "If you . . . , then I'm going to . . ."), a time or place where the threat may be carried out, the means by which the victim will be injured, and the intent of the threatener (e.g., "I might . . ." versus "I am going to . . ."). Also, the content of a threat can sometimes convey information about motive. Table 2.4 outlines examples of various psychological defenses organized according to their level of severity, a brief definition of the defense, and an example of a threatening statement or gesture that reflects the nature of the defensive process. This table is not exhaustive and merely provides a general framework for analyzing threatening statements with respect to their psychological significance.

An example may assist in illustrating how the content of a threat provided valuable information on the student's psychological state, which led to a helpful case management strategy. The youth was a twelve-year-old boy who had been teased excessively by other students for several months. He was an only child who never had many friends and was isolated from his peers. Although he did well aca-

TABLE 2.4. Relationship Between Level of Psychological Defense and Threatening Behaviors

Defense Mechanism	Definition	Threat Example
Humor (adaptive)	Uses amusing or ironic aspects of conflict.	"You're dead meat" (while laughing and playing game).
Self-Assertion (adaptive)	Expresses feelings or thoughts directly without coercion or manipulation.	"Don't pick on me!" (while pointing finger at someone).
Sublimation (adaptive)	Channels maladaptive feelings and thoughts into socially acceptable behavior.	Writes poetry, music, etc. with mildly aggressive themes; violence not gratuitous.
Devaluation (moderate)	Attributes exaggerated negative qualities to others.	"All jocks deserve death."
Intellectualization (moderate)	Uses abstract thinking or generalizations to control negative feelings.	Preoccupation with violent themes, but little or no emotion.
Omnipotence (moderate)	Feels or acts as though he or she has special powers.	"Death to all and I shall rule the world."
Autistic fantasy (severe)	Excessive daydreaming as a substitute for human relationships.	Bizarre or disorganized diary entries or journal writings involving violence; has no friends.
Psychotic distortion (severe)	Stress-induced break with reality leading to disorganized behavior or thinking.	In response to teasing, a quiet student abruptly yells, "Life is chaos and chaos is life. I shall bring about chaos."

demically, other students taunted him with claims of being "gay," "fat," and a "retard." Over a period of several months, his response to the teasing became increasingly more of a concern to school officials. On one occasion, he erupted in anger and smashed a chair, although he was mostly nonverbal and never talked to anyone about how he felt. His responses became more disorganized, and after an episode of rather intensive teasing, he erupted into a verbal tirade that frightened school officials and other students because of vague threatening statements he made and the seemingly disorganized quality of his speech. He stated, "Chaos is supreme. Chaos is life. Life is chaos. I will bring chaos." This disorganized statement communicated a vague threat, with an implied theme of omnipotence (i.e., "Chaos is supreme" and "I will bring chaos").

He was referred for further evaluation to determine his psychological stability and to make recommendations for management and treatment. The examination revealed pronounced narcissistic personality traits in which he was grandiose and viewed himself as superior to other students. This was a useful finding, because his social withdrawal initially led school officials to believe that he was socially inept and insecure. His narcissism led him to hide his emotions, but he erupted whenever his rage could no longer be contained. Moreover, although he showed no evidence of psychosis during most of the interview, when he was pressed about how other students treated him, his thinking showed some loosening of associations; psychological testing confirmed moderate disturbance in his thinking when placed under stress. He was referred for supportive psychotherapy and a psychiatric consultation to determine his suitability for treatment with medication. A recommendation was made for the school to monitor his behavior through regular meetings with his school guidance counselor. No other threatening or aggressive outbursts occurred for the remainder of the school year.

Although the content of a threat can reveal important information about the psychology of the threatener, such as motive and intent, other factors must be considered. Among these factors are issues related to the manner in which the threat is communicated.

HOW THREATS ARE COMMUNICATED

The intent to commit an act of violence is a private mental process that exists within the person who poses or is making the threat. Moreover, the true nature of this intention may or may not be expressed to others and the person may not want others to view a threat seriously, even though privately the person plans to carry it out. Therefore, it is difficult to know with complete certainty if the behavior of the person making a threat will match his or her stated intention. Likewise, an individual who intends to commit an act of violence may not always communicate his or her intention to others. In the Exceptional Case Study Project carried out by the United States Secret Service on individuals who had assassinated, attacked, or approached with lethal means a prominent public figure, Fein and Vossekuil (1999) found that 63 percent of their sample made an implicit or explicit threat about their target before the attack or approach. Moreover, threats were communicated to various individuals, including family, friends, co-workers, or other individuals who were known to the target. In other cases, threats were written in private diaries or journals. These findings suggest that individuals who pose a serious risk to a targeted victim frequently communicate their threats to another person.

In several recent school shootings, the perpetrators' violent intentions were communicated to peers and these threats were associated with an interest in violence and weapons (Verlinden, Hersen, and Thomas, 2000). In each of these cases, there was an apparent lack of concern by peers who knew the school assailants because they believed that the threats were not genuine. Moreover, peers failed to report these threats to family members, school officials, or professionals who were in a position to assist.

Threats are difficult to assess because they are often communicated to people who fail to warn authorities, which prevents appropriate protective measures from being taken. For example, a high school student who threatens to return to school the next day with a gun and "blow everyone away," may not be taken seriously by fellow classmates, and the threat may never be brought to the attention of school officials. Likewise, a student with strong negative views against a specific group who intends to commit a hate crime against a person or persons in that identified group (e.g., racial minorities, homosexuals) may communicate those views to other students who share similar beliefs. Consequently, a high likelihood exists that such threats will be communicated to others who endorse the individual's views and who sanction the intended violence. Therefore, selectively communicated threats are not likely to be brought to the attention of proper authorities.

Another difficulty is the issue of being able to recognize an actual threat. Recognizing the various ways in which threats can be expressed is an important aspect of threat assessment.

Written Communication

Direct or implied threats can be communicated in writing by students in many different ways. One of the more obvious ways is when a student writes a threatening letter or note and gives it to the intended victim. In these cases, the person making the threat can be readily identified if the message is signed or if the intended victim receives the message directly from the threatener. These cases are the clearest form of written communication. Other ways in which threats can be communicated in writing make identification of the threatener more difficult.

Sometimes the author of an anonymous note cannot be identified by the student receiving the threat. In some instances, information contained in the message makes identification possible. For example, if references to a situation have given rise to hostilities between two students, then inferences about the author can be drawn and investigated further. However, other forms of written communication make it difficult, if not impossible, to identify the threatener. Examples include anonymous threatening messages written on walls, blackboards, or other highly visible and accessible places. In these cases, another student may have observed the person writing the threatening message.

Threats may be communicated in writing through journal entries, diaries, and creative writings such as poetry or short stories. Such written expression is significant because these writings may not be made known to others and are not made public until after a violent incident has occurred. Prior to the school shooting in Oregon, Kip Kinkel frequently read from a personal journal in his English class about his plans to "kill everybody" (Verlinden, Hersen, and Thomas, 2000). Therefore, personal writings that convey a preoccupation with violence, threats against others, or gratuitous violence should be evaluated carefully and the student should be interviewed. The student's intentions to act on any violent thoughts or fantasies and his or her attitudes about violence as a means of resolving conflict should be explored.

Verbal Threats

Several variables can be evaluated when threats are expressed verbally, including the nature of the person to whom they are directed (i.e., intended victim versus third parties), whether the intended victim is indentified broadly (e.g., "Everyone must die") or specifically (e.g., "You are dead"), the seriousness of the intent, and whether the threat is accompanied by any gestures or actions. Sometimes the manner of verbal threats can be informative in determining the threatener's motivation. For example, a student who makes a verbal threat accompanied by a threatening gesture may be expressing emotions and regulating feelings of anger or rage. On the other hand, a student who repeatedly voices a series of threats only to another peer who also wishes to see the victim harmed may be planning a predatory act of violence in which a surprise attack is desired.

Verbal threats are difficult to document because no tangible evidence exists that can be recorded and retained for later analysis. Moreover, sometimes verbal threats are overheard by one or more individuals who make a retrospective report of the content. These reports may convey distorted, misperceived, or inaccurate recollections of the threat; if two or more individuals provide conflicting reports, the assessment is complicated by making the actual content of the threat unclear. Nevertheless, a comprehensive assessment of verbal threats should include collateral reports from others who have knowledge about the substance of and context in which the verbal threat was made.

Electronic Communication

Computers have revolutionized many aspects of the way we conduct our affairs. They are a part of the lives of children and adolescents in school settings. Indeed, many children and adolescents are more computer literate than their parents. Rapid development of the Internet over the past decade has enabled people to communicate with one another more readily and over larger distances. Although computers and the Internet are extremely valuable tools, they can also be used for making threats and other criminal activities.

Threatening communications can be made via computer in several ways. A student can send an e-mail message to another student, a teacher, or the school staff, and threatening messages can be posted on computer bulletin boards. Recently highly publicized cases cite an individual in a distant state who has made a vague or indirect threat to a person in another state. One of these cases involved a man in Florida who, after he began communicating with a student from Columbine High School in a computer chat room, threatened to "finish the job" started by the two youths who perpetrated the mass shooting at that school.

One of the challenges in examining threats made by computer is that the emotional tone, facial expressions, and other interpersonal features often used to determine one's psychological state cannot be assessed. If a student makes a threat such as, "I'm going to kill you," while joking around, interpersonal cues cannot be evaluated in electronic computer messages. Sometimes it is difficult to track the source of a threatening communication, and a computer technology specialist may be needed to help those responsible for evaluating electronically communicated threats determine the sender of the message.

Threats may be communicated electronically in other indirect ways. In one case, a student came to the attention of school officials after her behavior toward other students grew more provocative and insulting. She began to verbalize vague threats of wanting to assault other students. Through the evaluation process, it was discovered that she had her own Web page where she posted a "personal hit list" of other students whom she wanted dead. This threat was not initially known to school officials. A more thorough assessment was made of her feelings toward these specific students, the types of stressors and difficulties that contributed to her conflict with them, and her intentions behind posting this material in a public forum. This case illustrates that indirect or veiled threats can be communicated via computer in a variety ways, including e-mail, bulletin boards, and Web pages. Therefore, computer access and behavior should be explored in cases in which students exhibit potentially threatening behavior.

Symbolic Objects

Indirect threats can sometimes be communicated through the giving or sending of objects that have particular symbolic meaning for the threatener, victim, or both. These objects may have clear significance, as in drawings or pictures that have a violent or aggressive theme. For example, a male student sends his ex-girlfriend her photo torn in half, pasted on a sheet of paper, with a knife drawn between the two halves of the picture and drops of blood coming off the knife. This represents a fairly clear symbolic threat that may be either expressive, in which feelings of rage are being communicated, or instrumental, in which there is an intent to frighten the ex-girlfriend into considering a reconciliation. Other symbolic objects or images may convey threatening messages that are less clear and more equivocal, such as a student who sends another student a collage with themes of violence and death for reasons that are not entirely clear.

Symbolic objects do not necessarily have to be drawings or pictures; they can consist of bizarre, unusual, or inappropriate gifts that instill fear in the recipient. In some cases these symbolic objects or inappropriate gifts reflect an unusual or obsessive preoccupation with the victim or a bizarre expression of interest or attachment. When symbolic objects or inappropriate gifts are given, the assessment should focus on the meaning behind the symbolic object, including an assessment of the potential threatener's intent behind giving or sending the object and the meaning the object has for the recipient. Therefore, both the sender and recipient should be interviewed about these issues whenever possible.

Nonverbal Gestures

Many types of nonverbal behavior are intended to convey a threat or can be readily interpreted as a potential threat of violence. Depending on their context, these gestures range from fairly clear to equivocal or questionable threats of harm. Examples of nonverbal gestures that may constitute threats include the following: throat-slashing gestures; simulating a gun with one's fingers and shooting at someone; repeatedly brushing against someone in a forceful manner; pounding one's fist into one's hand; indicating an intent to physically attack a person; and pointing at someone as a means of intimidation.

Once again it is very important to fully evaluate the context in which nonverbal gestures occur because they may not be intended as a threat in certain situations. For example, the kindergartners in New Jersey who were playing "cops and robbers" and using their fingers as simulated guns were clearly not intending their nonverbal gestures to be threats outside the context of playing a game. Likewise, a middle school student who is talking about the banning of unsportsmanlike conduct in professional football with a group of peers and who is observed by a teacher to be using a throat-slashing gesture may be mistakenly believed to be threatening other students when that student is merely using the gesture to illustrate a point to others. On the other hand, a student who makes this gesture to another student with whom he or she has a conflict could be intending it as some form of threat.

THE RELATIONSHIP BETWEEN THREATS AND VIOLENCE

A direct relationship between a communicated threat and actual violence does not always exist. In some cases, the threat may be directly related to the potential for violence, as when a student communicates that he or she will commit an act of violence and then subsequently acts on the threat. The purpose of these kinds of threats is to induce fear in the victim as a way of increasing fear and suffering in the victim. Other cases involve threats that are only peripherally related to the violent act, as when threats represent one part of a broader pattern of acting-out behavior or aggression. In these cases, violence may be preceded by various acts of intimidation. Finally, threats may be completely unrelated to a specific act of violence. The student may threaten one specific act, only to commit a different act of violence at a later time.

Although research on the relationship between threats and violence is relatively scant, some studies suggest either no relationship or an inverse relationship between threats and violence. For example, Dietz, Matthews, van Duyne, and colleagues (1991) found that there was no relationship between express threats in letters to Hollywood celebrities and approach behavior directed toward the celebrity. In a related study, Dietz, Matthews, Martell, and colleagues (1991) found that there was an inverse relationship between threats and approach behavior toward members of the U.S. Congress. Likewise, although very few individuals in a sample of assassins and near-lethal approachers of public figures communicated a threat to the victim or law enforcement officers, many made their intentions known to someone they knew or in personal journals or writings (Fein and Vossekuil, 1999). This latter finding has been observed in a sample of school shooting assailants (Verlinden, Hersen, and Thomas, 2000), however, very little empirical research exists on the relationship between threats and violence among children and adolescents. However, as noted earlier and supported by the above findings, threatening behavior may or may not be predictive of violence in any given case. Therefore, the assessment and management of student threats requires an evaluation of several other factors related to violent behavior.

One common feature of both threats and violence is that they may vary in relative intensity or severity, depending on key factors such as the person's intent, situational variables, and proximity in time or distance between the threatener and intended victim. Monahan and Steadman (1996) outlined a system for reporting relative levels of risk for violence that vary along a continuum. They defined the first category of risk as *low violence risk,* in which very few factors increase the potential for violence. In these situations, no need for further assessment or preventive measures needs to be taken. The second category was defined as *moderate violence risk,* in which several risk enhancing factors may be present and additional assessment and monitoring of the individual are required. However, moderate levels of risk do not require immediate preventive measures other than monitoring or observation. The third category was defined as *high violence risk,* in which a number of factors raise the level of risk. These situations require the gathering of additional information, close monitoring of the person, and consideration of interventions such as civil commitment if the situation becomes more volatile. Finally, the fourth category was *very high violence risk,* in which many significant risk enhancing factors are present. In these situations, sufficient information exists to support preventive measures, such as warning potential victims, involuntary hospitalization, or intensive monitoring and treatment.

This general framework for categorizing levels of violence risk along a continuum according to the number or types of risk enhancing factors that are present and the imminence of danger can be applied to the classification of student threats in school settings (Mohandie, 2000). In other words, the relative level of risk present in a specific case can be delineated by applying general descriptive labels (i.e., low, moderate, high). In psychological measurement terms, this refers to an ordinal scale in which the relative order of levels of risk is important, ranging from low to high risk, but the degree of increase in danger is not necessarily the same from one level to the next. For example, a potentially threatening situation that escalates from low to moderate risk does not necessarily represent the same increase in risk as in a situation where moderate risk escalates to a high level of risk. An ordinal scale of measurement allows one to communicate relative, but not exact, levels of risk.

Another factor to consider is the number of risk levels needed to adequately present meaningful information about potential danger. Some professionals might favor an even number of points along a continuum to avoid having a middle point, while others favor an odd number of points to permit some middle ground. For example, the four levels of risk outlined by Monahan and Steadman (1996) (i.e., low, moderate, high, and very high) provide no middle point of risk, which may be viewed by some as desirable since evaluators may be drawn to assign middle levels of risk in cases in which a clear decision is difficult or the evidence of risk is equivocal. Nevertheless, five levels of risk for evaluating situations involving school threats are proposed here following the suggestion of Mohandie (2000). This allows professionals to consider a broader range of risk classification and to exhibit greater flexibility in terms of the types of interventions that may be considered.

The five levels of risk offered for classifying potential threats in school settings are as follows:

Level 1: Low Risk. No or minimal evidence exists that a student poses a threat of violence to other students. Regular educational programs should continue, and the student does not require any additional monitoring. No mental health or law enforcement intervention is necessary.

Level 2: Modest Risk. Some or equivocal evidence exists that a student poses a risk of harm to others, but there is no evidence of imminent intent, planning, or means for carrying out a threat. A referral for mental health services and some periodic monitoring may be needed, but no need is apparent for law enforcement intervention.

Level 3: Moderate Risk. Fairly clear evidence indicates that a student poses a risk of harm to others, and some evidence exists of planning, intent, or access to means, but these remain unclear. Regular monitoring and mental health assessment and treatment are indicated. The need for law enforcement intervention is not clear.

Level 4: High Risk. Clear evidence indicates that a student poses a risk of harm to others and evidence exists of planning, intent, and access to means for carrying out the threat. The student requires intensive supervision and monitoring and may require immediate mental health treatment, including possible involuntary hospitalization. Notification of law enforcement officials or potential victims may be necessary.

Level 5: Very High Risk. Clear and convincing evidence supports that a student poses an immediate risk of harm to others involving planning, intent, and an access to means. The student should be evaluated immediately for possible involuntary hospitalization; involvement of law enforcement officials is also required and notification of victims may be necessary.

Each of these approximate levels of risk for violence is based on a consideration of information from several different sources. It is important to remember that assignment of a particular level of risk in any one case does not remain a static and unchangeable finding. Because violence is a process and various situational variables can raise or lower relative risk, it may be necessary to conduct periodic assessments and to adjust the level of risk accordingly as risk-enhancing or risk-reducing factors change.

CONCLUSION

Several factors must be considered when evaluating the nature of aggressive and violent behavior, including the manner of expression (e.g., physical, verbal), motivation, and intent of the threatener. In addition, threats can be differentiated on several different dimensions, including the intended victim, threatener's intent, manner in which the threat is communicated, and clarity with which the threat is made. This chapter outlines several types of threats and dimensions that must be considered when conducting evaluations of threatening statements or communications by students. In addition, some guidelines are offered for evaluating the psychological state of the person making the threat and the general level of risk for violence that may exist in any given case. Aside from identifying the nature of the threat and attempting to clarify the threatener's motive and intentions, it is also necessary to consider other variables that are associated with a risk for violence. These issues are addressed in Chapter 3.

Chapter 3

Risk Assessment of Violent Behavior

One of the greatest challenges in evaluating school-based threats is determining which students truly pose a threat of violence and which do not. As noted earlier, not every student who makes a threat will actually become violent, and not every act of violence is preceded by a threat. In an ongoing study of forty cases involving school violence or shootings over the last twenty years, the United States Secret Service's National Threat Assessment Center has found that students who are prone to violence often do not make clear threats to victims or school officials, but instead make their intentions known to peers (Henry, 2000). Therefore, distinguishing between students who make a threat and those who actually pose a threat is a complicated process.

The assessment of violence potential requires careful analysis of specific variables that are associated with violent behavior. Although considerable debate has taken place as to whether professionals can predict an act of violence, the focus on prediction is misleading. Violence develops out of a complex interaction among characteristics of the perpetrator, victim, and situation. Furthermore, many psychological characteristics associated with violence are relatively stable, while others change over time. This is true for both perpetrators and victims. In addition, situational variables are sometimes predictable (e.g., knowing that someone in a temporary position will lose his or her job at a particular time), while others are not predictable (e.g., unexpected illnesses or accidents). Therefore, the changing quality of both situational and personal variables makes definitive prediction of violence difficult.

Nevertheless, significant advances have been made in our understanding of violent behavior that have emerged from the behavioral sciences. It is fair to say that an understanding of violent behavior requires careful analysis of psychological, social, environmental, biological, and situational factors that interact with one another. The research on correlates of violent behavior, including those factors that tend to increase or decrease a person's likelihood of committing a violent act, is a very useful resource upon which to draw for analyzing cases of probable student violence. Before examining this research, however, it is first necessary to conceptualize the process of violence risk assessment in terms of what it can and cannot contribute to the practice of assessing and managing threatening behavior in schools.

PREDICTION VERSUS RISK ASSESSMENT OF VIOLENCE

The empirical study of whether mental health professionals can accurately predict violence was formalized by Monahan's (1981) work in which he identified seven statistical correlates of violent behavior. These correlates included: a past history of violent crime; age (with violence rates higher among those in their late teens to early twenties); gender (with males more often violent than females); disadvantaged minority status; unemployment; and substance abuse. As additional risk factors for violence have been identified, they have typically been partitioned into *static* and *dynamic* classifications (Borum, 1996; Monahan and Steadman, 1994). Static risk factors for violence are those that do not change over time, such as gender and previous history of violence, or that change very little or slowly, including age or personality disorder diagnosis (Quinsey et al., 1998). Dynamic, or fluid, risk factors for violence are those that are situational or changeable, such as employment status, substance abuse, and medication noncompliance.

Two approaches can be used for predicting violence: *clinical* and *actuarial* (Garb, 1998; Grove and Meehl, 1996). Clinical approaches to violence risk assessment involve the collection of clinical data, history, and observations about an individual and the formulation of subjective impressions as to whether a person is potentially violent. The procedures used in this approach tend to be less systematic and thus more inconsistent across settings. Actuarial approaches to risk assessment are based on mathematically derived algorithms in which empirically established variables are systematically entered into an equation to yield a statistical probability that a person will or will not be violent. The advantages and disadvantages of both clinical and actuarial approaches have been discussed extensively in the literature

(Dawes, 1989; Dawes, Faust, and Meehl, 1989; Grove and Meehl, 1996). In general, research has revealed that actuarially based approaches to risk assessment are at least as good as, and usually better than, clinical approaches (Garb, 1998).

On the other hand, Litwack and Schlesinger (1999) pointed out that the distinction between clinical and actuarial approaches to determining violence potential is blurry because many actuarially based approaches require the input of information and data that call for clinical judgments. For example, Quinsey and his colleagues (1998) have developed an actuarial instrument, the Violence Risk Appraisal Guide (VRAG), that requires input of ratings for psychopathic personality characteristics, the presence or absence of schizophrenia, and the presence or absence of a personality disorder. Each of these variables is based on information derived from clinical assessments that require some expertise in psychiatric diagnosis. Therefore, clinical approaches to evaluating violence potential that are based on empirical findings and actuarial principles have a greater likelihood of accuracy and utility.

At the time Monahan (1981) conducted his review of the literature, he concluded that mental health professionals were correct only one out of three times in their predictions of violence. Since the publication of Monahan's review, however, considerable advances have been made in our understanding of the correlates of violence and in the ability of mental health professionals to make predictions about violent behavior. For example, Mossman (1994) demonstrated that mental health professionals perform better than chance when predicting violence, and Rice (1997) has outlined research showing considerable improvement in the prediction of sexual violence. A completely accurate method for predicting violent behavior, however, remains elusive.

In addition, much more is known about the demographic, clinical, and situational correlates of violence. Due in large measure to the multisite MacArthur Violence Risk Assessment research program (Steadman et al., 1998), additional risk factors have been identified, including psychopathic personality, frequency of prior arrests, hostility, violent fantasies, and substance abuse (Steadman et al., 2000).

Despite these recent advances mental health professionals have moved away from the conceptual framework of trying to offer definitive predictions of violent behavior. Instead, the more accepted approach is to undertake risk assessments of violent behavior, where an evaluation seeks to determine whether certain risk-enhancing and risk-reducing factors are present. The various ways in which findings from violence risk assessments are communicated can be used to illustrate the nature of this approach.

Heilbrun and colleagues (2000) examined the preferences of identified experts in violence risk assessment for communicating their findings. The preferred method for reporting opinions was identifying risk factors associated with violence that were applicable in a given case and providing recommendations for interventions that might reduce risk. An example would be concluding that heavy substance abuse in individuals with schizophrenia results in serious increases in their risk for violence and recommending that an inpatient substance abuse treatment program for dually diagnosed individuals be implemented. The second means of communicating risk that was preferred among psychologists was a qualified prediction in which a general classification of risk (i.e., high, moderate, low) was offered; among psychiatrists the second preferred method for communicating results was descriptive in which a patient's diagnosis, history, and clinical symptoms are reported. The least preferable method for communicating risk was a definitive statement in which a specific percentage of likelihood for violence (e.g., 70 percent) is cited.

These findings highlight the nature of risk assessment, as opposed to definitive prediction. In risk assessment, experts carefully analyze specific factors that are known to be associated with an increased risk for violence, as well as mitigating factors that reduce the likelihood of violence. The preferences of experts for communicating their results from violence risk assessments reflect a risk management, as opposed to a prediction-oriented model, for dealing with violence. According to Heilbrun (1997), prediction-oriented models are typically applied where a need exists to make definitive decisions about people, such as whether they should be involuntarily committed to a hospital, released on parole, or expelled from school. As such, prediction-oriented models are desired by individuals in legal settings and administrative positions. Risk management models focus on variables that raise or lower someone's potential for violence, as well as interventions directed at reducing the impact of risk-enhancing factors and increasing the strength of risk-reducing factors. Therefore, risk management strategies are suited in clinical settings where there is some control over the individual and the person's response to treatment can be monitored.

Based on this analysis, a risk management model of violence risk assessment is best suited for school settings. Rather than attempting to definitively predict violence among students, as many school staff and mental health professionals feel pressure to do, a risk management model focuses instead on various risk-enhancing and risk-reducing factors associated with violence and seeks to produce a constructive plan for managing risk. Many principles of violence risk assessment can be applied to the evaluation of threats and potentially violent situations in schools, provided the identification of risk is viewed as one step rather than the result in the process.

More specifically, the assessment phase should include a detailed outline of those factors that increase a student's risk for violence and the specific nature of those factors, such as whether they are stable (e.g., history of violence, family history of criminality) or dynamic (e.g., substance abuse, periodic teasing by peers). Once all of the relevant factors have been outlined, then management strategies for dealing with each factor can be developed. To facilitate this process, a brief overview of factors associated with the risk for violence in children and adolescents will be outlined. Before proceeding, however, it is necessary to clarify some situations where a risk management model may come into conflict with demands for a prediction-oriented model for dealing with violence.

PERSONAL SECURITY VERSUS COMMUNITY POLICING

One demand that school officials and mental health professionals who work in school settings encounter from parents, school board members, and politicians is to provide a safe and secure environment in which children can learn. This pressure may be direct or implied and often a need exists to lend the appearance that something is being done to deal with school violence. Competing needs from different interest groups sometimes make efforts toward dealing with school violence difficult to establish in a balanced and equitable fashion that satisfies everyone. On the one hand, parents of children who are being victimized may call for the expulsion of an offending student; on the other hand, administrative concerns or pressure from parents of those students who have been identified as aggressive may preclude certain actions, such as expulsion, from being taken without a clear and present danger to others.

Some of these issues are compounded by the notion that violence can be predicted. For example, personal security experts have outlined so-called "warning signs" that are intended to serve as cues of potential danger in one's environment (de Becker, 1997). Although many compelling case examples cite how a person used intuition to avoid a potentially dangerous or deadly situation, this approach to assessing and managing violence is better suited for personal protection than for establishing a program within the school or community. The reason is that many anecdotal cases where people have subjectively or intuitively avoided violence provides support not for *pre*diction, but for *post*diction (McCann, 2001). That is, it is easy to examine causal factors of violence in cases in which violence has already occurred; but in everyday situations in which outcomes are not yet known, the critical concern is what may happen in the future and what can be done to protect others.

Personal security measures that are based on looking for "warning signs" for potential danger are more readily applicable to individuals in their personal lives. For example, if a student starts dating someone that his or her parents do not like for unspecified reasons (e.g., "I just don't like him") or based on generalizations that may be unfounded (e.g., "I don't like the clothes he wears"), any errors in judgment that this person is dangerous are likely to result in the student not dating the person. However, no major personal intrusions occur for the person about whom the judgments are made. If these same approaches to prediction are applied in a school setting (e.g., students who are "not liked" by administrators; certain clothing is banned for fear that it will provoke violence) then many students may be unfairly targeted as potentially violent.

Many agencies and school districts circulate information on "warning signs" to which parents, teachers, and others should be attuned. These warning signs are often used to identify students who might pose a risk of violence to others. Some of these indicators of violence are clearly important and should be evaluated further, such as a student making a threat, bringing a weapon to school, or being preoccupied with violence and aggression. However, other "warning signs" for violence that have been circulated include indicators of general psychological disturbance that by themselves do not provide unique information about violent behavior, such as poor peer relationships, feelings of anger or frustration, and being economically disadvantaged.

Therefore, the tension arises between a need for personal protection, when parents, students, and other family members have a principal goal of keeping a student safe from violence, and the desire not to unfairly target students as potentially violent. If protective measures result in some students being identified as potentially violent, yet those students never become violent, personal protection advocates view this as an acceptable cost for keeping students safe. On the other hand, the needs and interests of each student are concerns, and the goal is to provide a safe and secure environment by using policies and procedures that are legally permissible, fair, and which minimize errors in judgment. Therefore, the use of "warning signs," or the formulation of "profiles" of the potentially violent student, do not lend themselves well to the assessment and management of threatening and potentially violent situations, except to the extent that these warning signs and profiles provide relevant information for understanding risk factors that can be evaluated further.

CORRELATES OF VIOLENT BEHAVIOR IN YOUNG PEOPLE

The formal practice of clinical risk assessment does not lend itself readily to evaluating and managing threats in schools, primarily because violent behavior is a relatively low base rate phenomenon and inherent challenges exist in differentiating students who pose a threat from those who do not. Nevertheless, research on risk factors associated with violence provides information that can and should be used in the evaluation of situations in which a student has made a threat or is believed to pose a threat of violence.

Hawkins and colleagues (1998) provide a comprehensive review of risk factors for youth violence. These researchers reviewed individual research studies on five groups of risk factors associated with violence: (1) individual, (2) family, (3) school, (4) peer, and (5) community and neighborhood factors.

Individual risk factors for violence were differentiated by Hawkins and colleagues (1998) into medical/physical conditions and psychological characteristics. Among medical/physical conditions, maternal pregnancy and birth complications are inconsistently related to youth violence and any positive statistical relationships that have been observed are typically regarded as weak. Another physical variable that has been studied is low resting heart rate. Once again, evidence is inconclusive as to whether a low resting heart rate is predictive of youth violence. The theory that heart rate may be associated with violent behavior is based on the notion that a low resting heart rate reflects underarousal, which reduces the capacity for experiencing the anxiety that would inhibit acting out, resulting in a fearless temperament (Raine, 1993). Biological factors that have been shown to increase the risk for aggressive and violent acting out include a history of head injury, particularly frontal lobe injury, infectious diseases that affect the central nervous system, and increased testosterone (Brewer et al., 1995). However, these factors may reflect a preresponse tendency toward violence that lowers an individual's frustration tolerance and results in higher levels of impulsivity. The presence of any of these risk factors does not guarantee that a specific youth will act violently, and situational factors also play a critical role in determining when and under what circumstances a youth with specific biological predispositions will engage in violence (Geen, 1998). Medical and biological factors are important to consider and should be evaluated as part of a comprehensive evaluation, but they should not be viewed apart from situational factors.

Substance abuse has also been identified as a factor that increases violence potential (Brewer et al., 1995). Acute alcohol intoxication can precipitate aggression through disinhibition and reduction of impulse controls. Stimulant (e.g., amphetamines, cocaine) intoxication results in severe psychomotor agitation that can result in aggression, and hallucinogens (e.g., LSD, PCP) alter perceptual states and may result in markedly impaired judgment that can lead to violent behavior. Some drug-induced mental states, particularly when consumption has been heavy, may result in acute psychotic episodes that involve paranoid or grandiose delusions. Therefore, an important component in assessing students who either make or pose a threat is to evaluate their patterns of substance abuse, including the types and frequency of drugs used, as well as the behavioral effects of specific substances.

Several psychological variables have been studied as potential risk factors for violence in young people. One cluster of symptoms that has shown a significant relationship to violence is associated with attention deficit hyperactivity disorder (Barkley, 1997, 1998). More specifically, hyperactivity, problems with sustaining attention, impulsivity, and risk-taking behavior have all been associated with a heightened risk for violence (Hawkins et al., 1998). Psychological evaluations of students who come to the attention of school officials due to threatening behavior or concerns about violence potential should include screening for attention deficit hyperactivity disorder.

Hawkins and colleagues (1998) have also identified a number of other psychological variables that are associated with an increased risk for violent acting out in young people. Children who exhibit violent or criminal behavior at an early age are at much greater risk for continuing their violence into adolescence. Moreover, the early onset of violent and criminal behavior "is associated with greater seriousness and chronicity of violence" (Hawkins et al., 1998, p. 132). In addition, the greater versatility a male youth shows in his criminal or delinquent behavior, including stealing, selling drugs, vandalism, and other behavioral or conduct problems, the greater the likelihood that he will engage in violent behavior. Aggressive behavior, such as bullying, hitting, or physical intimidation, is also associated with higher levels of violence. One set of variables that has not shown a significant association with violent behavior in children and adolescents is internalizing disorders, which are defined by high levels of anxiety, worry, or social withdrawal.

Also examined with respect to their relationship to violence potential in young people are the youth's family environment and quality of relationships among family members. One particular issue that has been examined is the relationship between a history of child physical or sexual abuse and the potential for later violence. Although some relationship between child abuse and violence is apparent, according to Hawkins and colleagues (1998), this relationship is modest, and child neglect appears to be a stronger predictor of later violence than other forms of maltreatment.

Several factors in the relationship between a child and his or her parents are related to violent acting out. When parents do not give their children clear expectations, supervise their children inconsistently or minimally, and provide inconsistent or extremely harsh discipline, children are at much greater risk for delinquent behavior and substance abuse. Moreover, children are at a greater risk for violence when their parents do not have much involvement with them and are not an active part of their lives. Other family variables that also increase the risk for later violence include: high levels of parental conflict in the home; parents expressing favorable attitudes toward violence as a means of resolving conflict; and early disruptions in the parent-child relationship resulting from abandonment, children leaving home before the age of sixteen, or removal of the children from the home.

Some factors believed to be related to violence among children have not received strong empirical support, including a parental history of criminal behavior or arrests, stressful family events, and frequent moving of the family residence. For example, one study found a modest relationship between a history of parental arrests prior to the child reaching age ten and self-reported violence in adolescence (Farrington, 1989). However, another study found no relationship between these two variables (Moffitt, 1987). Raine (1993) has pointed to research that suggests the strongest correlation between parental criminality and delinquency in children and youths is for property crimes, particularly burglary. Familial factors that contribute the most to an increased likelihood of violent behavior in the children and adolescents is parental attitudes that endorse violent and aggressive behavior as an acceptable means of coping with interpersonal difficulties.

School factors are a third major set of variables that have been studied with respect to their relationship to violent behavior among children and adolescents. Among the strongest predictors of violence are early academic difficulties, poor achievement, truancy, and quitting school prior to age fifteen (Farrington, 1989; Hawkins et al., 1998). Factors related to school that have shown an inconsistent relationship to future violence include the strength of attachment or connectedness a student has to school and frequent school transitions. Hawkins and colleagues (1998) pointed out that these inconclusive findings suggest that the more important questions to ask include: "Why does a student not feel connected to school?" and "What factors have contributed to frequent changes in schools?" It may be that disrupted family relationships or psychological disturbances in the child or parents are stronger contributors to violent behavior.

Research also suggests that a bond or commitment to school can serve as a protective factor against violence by reducing a student's propensity to act out aggressively (Verlinden, Hersen, and Thomas, 2000). In particular, this research suggests that prior to age ten, bonding or connectedness to school is not related to later violence, whereas the relationship does become significant between ages fourteen and sixteen. Once again, further research is needed to elucidate whether it is school connectedness or other related factors, such as stability of the adolescent's social environment, that account for these observed relationships.

The fourth major set of variables that have been studied with respect to their impact on a child or adolescent's risk for violence is peer relationships. Several variables show a strong association with a propensity for violence, such as having siblings who engage in delinquent behavior, having peers who are antisocial, and being a member of a gang (Hawkins et al., 1998). Compared to children and adolescents who are not members of gangs or those who are not closely associated with peer groups that endorse violence, gang members have much higher rates of serious and violent delinquency and are responsible for most delinquent acts despite the fact that they are relatively fewer in number (Thornberry, 1998). Critical variables that require careful analysis when evaluating student threats are the nature of the student's peer group, the extent of the peers' delinquency, membership in an organized group or gang, and norms and attitudes about violence within the student's significant peer group.

The fifth set of factors that has been studied with respect to its relationship to violence in youths is community and situational conditions. Monahan (1981) identified several major correlates of violent behavior, including environmental factors, such as unemployment and economic disadvantage. Among children and adolescents, similar factors have been identified as being associated with an increased risk for violence. These factors include living in conditions of poverty, community disorganization, a lack of cohesiveness in the youth's neighborhood, availability of drugs, the presence of neighborhood adults who are involved in crime, exposure to community violence, and experiencing racial prejudice (Hawkins et al., 1998). In addition, situational factors are also associated with an increased risk for violence, including substance abuse and the availability of weapons.

Another approach to studying violence risk among children and adolescents is to examine several variables concurrently to determine if multivariate models of prediction can provide useful information on how these various factors interact. For example, Ellickson and

McGuigan (2000) conducted a multivariate analysis of early predictors of violence in adolescence. They found that a history of doing poorly in school, early delinquent or deviant behavior, and male gender were the strongest predictors of violence by the end of high school. Students who went to several elementary schools and who attended middle schools with high levels of drug use among peers were more likely to become violent in high school. Low self-esteem was also a predictor of both predatory and relational violence, while greater maturity served as a protective factor against violence that occurred within the context of interpersonal relationships. In addition, relational and predatory violence each had unique predictive factors. Relational violence in high school, defined as aggression occurring in the context of personal conflict, was predicted by a student having attended two or more elementary schools and a middle school with high levels of drug use. Predatory violence was predicted by a student's early drug use and high levels of drug use among his or her peers in middle school.

In addition, some research on the correlates of violent behavior in children and adolescents has focused specifically on neurobiological factors, such as abnormal serotonin and other neurotransmitter metabolism (Schalling, 1993; Virkkunen and Lonnoila, 1993; Volavka, 1995). Although this research holds considerable promise for increasing our understanding of the causes of violence, it does not have direct clinical application. For instance, whether changes in neurotransmitter levels are a cause or consequence of violent behavior, or if both violence and neurochemical changes are due to a third variable remains unclear. Moreover, no practical means exist for evaluating neurotransmitter levels in applied settings, such as schools. Although this research will not be discussed further, professionals are encouraged to evaluate biological and medical factors that can be more directly evaluated and that impact a student's potential for violence, such as a history of serious head injury, the presence of a seizure disorder, substance abuse, and developmental conditions (e.g., mental retardation, developmental disorders).

VIOLENCE AND MENTAL DISORDER

Study of the relationship between violence and mental disorder is complicated by several factors. For one thing, the use of psychiatric diagnostic classifications, such as schizophrenia or major mood disorders, are essentially designed to facilitate mental health assessment and treatment, not to evaluate and predict violent behavior (Shah, 1993). In addition, diagnostic classifications are heterogeneous categories, which means that people who have the same disorder may differ from one another in terms of severity, the presence of specific symptoms, and environmental supports or stressors that impact how the mental disorder is manifested. The controversial issue of whether mentally ill individuals are more dangerous than people without a major mental illness remains. Link and Stueve (1994) present data illustrating some relationship between mental disorder and violence, although broad diagnostic categories are not particularly informative. It appears to be more informative to look at specific symptoms of mental disorders, rather than individual diagnostic categories, to more accurately understand this relationship.

Another issue that complicates the study of the relationship between mental disorder and violence, particularly among children and adolescents, is that some severe psychiatric disturbances, such as schizophrenia and major mood disorders, have their onset in adulthood. Therefore, the prevalence of these conditions is lower in younger individuals and systematic research on these conditions, particularly with respect to violence, is limited. Other psychiatric disorders that have their onset in childhood or adolescence, such as conduct disorder and attention deficit hyperactivity disorder, have been the focus of study. However, some symptoms associated with these conditions overlap with other factors shown to be associated with violence in young people, such as a history of academic problems, early onset of delinquency, and impulsivity. The issue of whether severe psychiatric disturbances, such as delusions, hallucinations, thought disorder, or serious mood disturbances, are related to violence in young people still remains.

It is worth reviewing some major findings on the relationship between serious mental disorder and violence because the presence of certain symptoms should alert the examiner to the need for further assessment. Some symptoms (e.g., command auditory hallucinations, paranoid delusions) have sufficient face validity as a risk factor for violence that they need to be explored fully when assessing threatening behavior among students.

The relationship between serious mental disorder and violent behavior has been studied by looking at the prevalence of psychiatric disorders among subgroups of violent and nonviolent individuals, as well as by looking at the prevalence of violent behavior among individuals with and without a serious mental disorder. According to data presented by Swanson (1994), people who assaulted another person were about 2.5 to 4.0 times more likely to have a psychiatric disorder such as schizophrenia, major mood disorder, or an anxiety disorder. Similarly, there was a higher rate of violent behavior among those with a serious mental disorder, compared to those without a psychiatric diagnosis. However, Swanson pointed out that the major portion of violence among individuals with a mental disorder was accounted for by the co-occurrence of serious psychiatric illness and substance abuse. This finding has also been observed in the findings of Steadman and his colleagues (1998) in which the rate of violent behavior was greatest among those individuals with a serious mental disorder who also abused drugs or alcohol. Thus, a significant risk factor for violent behavior exists in those individuals with a serious mental disorder who also are abusing substances.

Specific symptoms of serious mental disturbance and variables associated with their presentation are more important in assessing violence potential than the mere presence or absence of a mental disorder diagnosis. For instance, Link and Stueve (1994) note that threat/control override symptoms create an increased risk for violence, independent of other symptoms of psychosis. Threat/control override symptoms are associated with a belief that one's internal controls are being overridden by some external force. Examples include feeling that one's thoughts are being controlled by outside forces (e.g., thought stealing), believing that thoughts are being inserted into one's head against that person's will (e.g., thought insertion), and feeling that others are out to harm the person (e.g., paranoid delusions). Although research has provided support for the relationship between threat/control override symptoms and violence, recent findings suggest that this relationship must be studied more fully (Steadman et al., 2000). Nevertheless, the presence of threat/control override symptoms, paranoid ideation, and other symptoms that reflect an exaggerated sense of personal attack or threat should be evaluated in students who may pose a risk of violence to others.

Other symptoms that require further assessment are hallucinations (McNeil, 1994) and delusions (Taylor et al., 1994). According to Monahan (1993), an additional factor that must be considered with respect to symptoms of psychosis is whether hallucinations and delusions are active or in remission. When psychiatric patients are in a florid phase of their illness, the disorganization that occurs in their thinking and behavior, as well as impairment in their judgment, leads to an increased risk for violence. In a related way, medication noncompliance is associated with an increased risk for violence among psychiatric patients. When patients fail to follow through on their prescribed course of treatment, they are at risk of decompensation, which leads to more active and florid states of psychosis that can increase the risk for violence.

Students who are being evaluated on their potential for violence, and who have a serious mental disorder should be evaluated with respect to the specific symptoms they exhibit; hallucinations, delusions, and the course of these symptoms should all be assessed. Particular attention should also be paid to the content of the hallucinations and delusions. Command auditory hallucinations, in which the student perceives a voice giving him or her instructions to act in a particular manner, including directions to commit an act of violence, should be evaluated with respect to how the student views the voice, whether the student feels compelled to act on the voice, prior instances when the student may have obeyed the voice, methods used to distract attention away from the voice, and factors that seem to increase or decrease the intensity of the voice. Similarly, a delusion should be evaluated with respect to whether its content is related to hallucinations, the willingness of the student to consider that the delusion may not be true, and other factors that reflect how a delusion may control the student's behavior.

Although substance abuse is an independent factor that increases the risk for violence, the presence of alcohol or drug abuse in a student who also has a serious mental disorder requires very careful consideration. The co-occurrence of substance abuse and serious mental disorder in a student should be considered a significant risk-enhancing factor, and interventions should be directed at addressing both problems.

Several mental disorders that are first diagnosed in childhood or adolescence may have some relationship to violent behavior. Among the more relevant conditions are Asperger's syndrome and those disorders in the DSM-IV that are classified as disruptive behavior disorders, namely conduct disorder, oppositional defiant disorder, and attention deficit hyperactivity disorder.

Asperger's syndrome is a condition that is similar to autism and is characterized by pervasive and chronic impairment in the child's social interaction, as well as impaired development in behavioral interests and activities (American Psychiatric Association, 1994). Among the major features of Asperger's syndrome are marked solitary behavior, a lack of interest in social relationships, lack of empathy, poor recognition of social cues (e.g., smiling, poor eye contact), a lack of spontaneity, preoccupation with stereotypic or unusual interests, repetitive mannerisms, and inflexibility. This syndrome has a developmental course that extends into adulthood and is closely related to schizoid personality disorder, which is also characterized by a lack of social interest, poor spontaneity in social relationships, and barren emotionality. According to Maughan (1993), individuals with Asperger's syndrome appear no more likely than other individuals with mental disorders to display violent or aggressive behavior. However, Maughan noted that violent behavior in those children and adolescents with this condition has a unique quality: these violent and aggressive outbursts are often unusual, abrupt, unpredictable, and possibly associated with an unusual fantasy life. In addition, parents and family members are often targets of unprovoked attacks, which seem to be precipitated by the individual's perception that the behavior of others is intrusive.

Students who have Asperger's syndrome or display a schizoid personality style or pattern and who are believed to present a potential risk for violence should be evaluated with respect to several factors: private fantasies and thoughts should be explored, and the response of these students should also be examined in other situations where others may have been intrusive.

The presence of oppositional defiant disorder in a child or adolescent may create a heightened risk for violence or aggression, depending on a student's potential for acting out. Once again, it is important to focus on the specific symptoms that are present, rather than the presence or absence of the diagnosis. Oppositional defiant disorder is characterized by a pattern of negative, hostile, and defiant behavior that includes temper tantrums, frequent arguing, active defiance of rules, provoking others, blaming others for personal problems, irritability, anger, and vindictive behavior (American Psychiatric Association, 1994). These symptoms reveal that students with this disorder are prone to be angry, hostile, and vengeful. Therefore, an increased risk for violence exists, depending on situational factors that may trigger an aggressive outburst. In addition, the behaviors of children and adolescents with this disorder suggest that they may be more prone to endorse negative or oppositional attitudes, including a more positive view of aggression or violence as an appropriate means of coping with conflict.

Conduct disorder in children and adolescents is characterized by a pattern of behavior in which the rights of others are violated. Specific symptoms of this condition include bullying, threatening behavior, use of a weapon, physical cruelty, stealing, cruelty to animals, forced sexual activity, destruction of property, lying, and truancy (American Psychiatric Association, 1994). In addition, conduct disorder has been shown to be a significant factor that increases the risk for violence and criminality (Robins, 1993). Moreover, constructs related to conduct disorder are antisocial personality disorder in adults and psychopathy (Hare, 1991; Hare and Hart, 1993). Although some conduct disturbances in juveniles are limited to childhood and adolescence, and other patterns of conduct disturbance persist over the life course into adulthood (Moffitt, 1993), the presence of conduct disorder in a child or adolescent who comes to the attention of school officials as a possible threat to others should alert examiners to a heightened risk for violence.

Another important factor to consider is the degree of psychopathic personality disturbance a youth may exhibit. Psychopathy is a distinct personality disturbance that overlaps with, but is not equivalent to, antisocial personality disorder. The major features of psychopathy include the following: superficial charm; grandiose self-worth; need for stimulation and proneness to boredom; pathological lying; manipulation; lack of guilt or remorse; shallow affect; lack of empathy; lifestyle in which others are taken advantage of; poor behavioral controls; promiscuous sexual behavior; early behavior problems; lack of realistic long-term goals; impulsivity; irresponsibility; failure to accept responsibility for one's actions; juvenile delinquency; revocation of a conditional release; and involvement in many different types of criminal behavior (Hare, 1991). The presence of psychopathy has been reliably identified in male juvenile offenders (Forth, Hart, and Hare, 1990), and this variable has been shown to result in a significant increase in risk for violent behavior. Therefore, characteristics associated with psychopathy should be examined in students who are being evaluated.

As noted earlier, the presence of attention deficit hyperactivity disorder has also been identified as a factor associated with an increased risk for violence. This disorder is characterized by problems with inattention (e.g., failure to keep on task, failure to listen to instructions, difficulty organizing, distractibility), hyperactivity-impulsivity (e.g., fidgeting, difficulty sitting still, interrupting, difficulty awaiting turn), or a combination of both inattention and hyperactivity-impulsivity. According to research reviewed by Volavka (1995), the presence of attention deficit hyperactivity disorder is associated with an increased risk for both noncriminal and criminal violence. Several possible reasons exist for how this condition is associated with violence, including the fact that attention deficit hyperactivity disorder leads to other problems associated with violence. These resultant problems may include poor peer relationships, academic failure, impulsivity, and weak social and school bonds. Once again, any diagnostic or mental health evaluation that occurs within the context of a threat assessment should screen for symptoms of attention deficit hyperactivity disorder.

Finally, other mental disorders that may exacerbate or lead to other risk factors for violence should be considered. For instance, the presence of mental retardation, borderline intellectual functioning, a specific learning disability, and developmental disorders, while not necessarily indicative of an increased risk for violence in every case, may lead to other problems that play a role in understanding a student's potential for violence. More specifically, these conditions result in academic maladjustment, social alienation or shunning by peers, poor coping resources, and difficulty modulating emotions effectively. Therefore, they should be considered in the mental health evaluation component of a threat assessment.

CONCLUSION

It is difficult to apply specific risk factors for violence in a clinically useful way because violence is a process that is based on a complex interaction of individual and situational factors. As mentioned previously, actuarial models for predicting violence are generally as good as, and often superior to, approaches based solely on clinical judgment. Although actuarial models are being developed to improve the prediction of violent behavior in clinical and forensic settings, application of these models is difficult when evaluating threats in nonclinical settings such as schools or the workplace. A major reason for this limitation is that violence is a low base rate behavior and actuarial approaches for evaluating threatening communications are nonexistent.

Given the situational nature of threatening and violent behavior and the interdisciplinary nature of threat assessment, reliance on any single predictor severely limits the likelihood that threatening situations can be managed effectively. In the next chapter, a comprehensive approach to evaluating threats will be presented, based on an integration of psychological, social, and situational risk factors associated with violent behavior.

Chapter 4

Assessing and Evaluating Threats

The process of threat management is intended to prevent violent acts and assure safety and security for students in educational settings. However, effective management of threats is largely dependent on accurate identification and assessment of threatening or potentially violent situations. One of the most challenging issues facing individuals who undertake the role of evaluating and managing threats is determining how potentially dangerous individuals or situations are identified and referred for a more thorough assessment. What makes identification difficult is that there are no error-free, definitive methods for determining who will and who will not become violent in any given situation.

Grisso (1998) has pointed out that the process of evaluating violence potential in children and adolescents must be guided not only by specific factors that raise or lower risk, but also by an awareness of the potential sources of error in judgments about violence potential among young people. More specifically, Grisso suggests that professionals should refrain from offering definitive predictions of whether a particular youth will or will not become violent and should instead attend to relevant risk-enhancing and risk-inhibiting factors, as well as the social context in which the youth is placed. For example, an assessment of violence potential should be framed according to the following general framework: If the youth remains in the school setting, without appropriate supports, the risk for violence is (low, moderate, high, very high). If the youth remains in the school setting and receives intensive individual psychotherapy, a change in class schedule, and regular behavioral monitoring, the risk for violence is . . . If the youth is placed in a structured residential treatment program, the risk for violence is . . . Identification of various situational factors that increase risk for violence (e.g., persistent peer teasing, substance abuse) should also be delineated. Overall, it is important to recognize that contextual factors must be referenced when assessing threats, and great diversity exists in the causes, motives, and triggers of violent behavior in young people.

Because situational factors influence whether a specific student will become violent, another critical and controversial issue must be recognized with respect to the identification and assessment of potentially violent students. One debated approach to managing school violence is the use of profiling techniques to identify potentially dangerous or violent students. Kinney (1996) has pointed out the problems with profiling in his discussion of threat management in workplace settings; however, his comments are very applicable to the problem of profiling students in schools:

> There is a tendency to compare the behavioral characteristics and features of those individuals to whom threats have been attributed with the personal characteristics of those who previously committed acts of violence. Undue emphasis on the use of profiles can be harmful for many reasons. For openers, there are many individuals who are likely to have some of the characteristics of past perpetrators. Because these individuals fit a profile does not mean that they will become violent. (p. 305)

This analysis points out that certain characteristics may indicate violence potential in some respects, in that they are found among students who commit a violent act, but these same characteristic are not necessarily specific because they are also present in some students who will not become violent. Therefore, profiling of students runs the risk of erroneously attributing a potential for violence to those individuals who may never become violent, thus stigmatizing certain students. In addition, Kinney (1996) has noted that focusing on the type of people who commit violence, rather than on behaviors and situations that lead to violence, may divert attention from those people or situations that pose a serious threat. If behavioral or psychological profile data are to be used at all in the threat assessment process, they should be applied only to the extent that they highlight variables that should be considered in the overall evaluation and only in the latter stages of assessment and management process, once a student or situation has been identified.

Rather than be guided by profiles, a more effective approach to identifying and assessing student threats or violence potential is to focus on behaviors and situational factors that are associated with the sequence of escalating aggression or violence. According to Kinney (1996), violent acts emerge from a series of acts and conditions that should be the focus of attention. This sequence begins when an individual experiences some stressor or a series of stressors that cause tension and anxiety. Thereafter, the person begins to feel that these problems are unsolvable and that other people or situations are responsible for personal problems. The person becomes more self-absorbed, and self-protective motivations begin to take over the person's thinking, which in turn leads to the person viewing violence as the only means of coping with problems and protecting oneself. The sequence of violence that Kinney (1996) has outlined is similar to the notion set forth by Fein and Vossekuil (1998) that violence is a process based on the individual characteristics of the perpetrator and victim, as well as situational and contextual factors. Assessment of threatening and potentially violent behavior in school settings should be based on a process-oriented approach, rather than one that is based on trying to profile individual students who may be potentially violent. In a process-oriented approach, the focus is on behavior, patterns of behavior, and situational factors.

In this chapter, various methods for assessing student threats and potentially violent situations are outlined. Some student threats may be overt and clearly stated, whether or not they are accompanied by an intent to carry out the threat; therefore, direct methods of assessment such as examining the threatener's motive, intent, and credibility are possible. In addition, specific issues must be evaluated, such as a student's access to weapons, a prior history of violence, substance abuse, and other factors that are associated with violence potential. However, some students who pose a threat do not necessarily communicate their plans to the victim or to school officials and, therefore, indirect methods for identifying behavioral patterns associated with violence risk must also be considered. Factors that tend to inhibit or reduce the potential for violence must also be assessed. This chapter reviews these issues and closes with a brief discussion of interdisciplinary approaches that can facilitate the threat assessment process.

DIRECT QUESTIONS TO ASK ABOUT A THREAT

Several factors should be evaluated directly when appraising the nature of threats made by students in school settings, including whether the student intends to carry out the threat, to whom the threat was communicated, the imminent nature of the risk for violence, and related factors. A number of basic questions should be formulated about the threat at the start of the assessment process.

What is the content or nature of the threat?

If a student has made a threatening communication, the first step is to focus on the content of the message. More specifically, the threatened action should be specified (e.g., arson, bombing, robbery, murder, physical assault) as well as the specific victim or victims to be targeted and how the threat is to be carried out. If a student has not made a specific threatening statement, but is nevertheless believed to pose a threat, then the various forms of violence or aggression that are suspected should be outlined. For instance, if a student has a long history of physical fights, intimidation, bullying, and other forms of interpersonal aggression, then these past behaviors may constitute the types of actions that should be of concern.

Some appraisal of the violence with which the victim has been threatened should take place. Sometimes a violent act is not specified, in the case of veiled, nonspecific, or expressive threats (e.g., "Someone is going to pay"), which may be a reflection of either the threatener's emotional state or the degree of planning and forethought (or lack thereof) the student has given to carrying out the threat. It is important to obtain as much information as possible about the suspected violence, including dates, times, and conditions under which and the means by which the threatened violent act will be carried out (e.g., with or without a weapon). Efforts should also be directed at determining whether the student has either planned or gained access to a means for carrying out the threat (e.g., having access to handguns, downloading bomb recipes from the Internet).

What is the intent of the threatener?

This question is a crucial but often challenging factor to evaluate because the true intent of a person making a threat is the major variable that determines whether a threat will be carried out. However, the private nature of thoughts and intentions often make it impossible to know with complete certainty if a person intends to carry out an act. Some individuals may threaten an act of violence merely to induce fear and intimidate the victim, but they have no intention of becoming violent. In other cases, a student may intend to harm another person or commit an act of violence but this intent is not communicated to anyone.

The content of a threatening communication can provide some insight into the threatener's intent. Careful attention to the language, particularly verb tenses used by the threatener, is one means of evaluating intent. The use of definitive language, such as "I will . . ." or "I am going to . . .", conveys greater intent to carry out a threat. Likewise, terms that reveal definitive action (e.g., "Definitely," "You can count on . . .") should also be taken as evidence in support of the hypothesis that the student intends to carry out a threat. Although definitive language does not necessarily mean that the threat will be carried out ultimately, it is one piece of evidence as to the threatener's intention.

Intent must also be inferred based on a comprehensive analysis of the context in which a threat is made, the nature of the victim, and secondary gain. Efforts by the perpetrator to conceal plans for violence suggest an intent to avoid detection and increase the likelihood of success. In short, the threatener's intent must be inferred after carefully analyzing all relevant factors related to how, why, and to whom a threat has been communicated.

What does the threatener wish to convey?

This question addresses something different than whether the threatener intends to carry out the threat. A related but slightly different consideration in evaluating a threat is to establish whether the threatener wishes to have his or her threat taken seriously. The person making a threat may have certain expectations about how others will perceive the threat, independent of whether any intention exists of carrying it out. For instance, a student making a threat may have no intention of being violent, even though he or she may want the threat to be taken seriously. Using a threat only, with no planned violence, the student may want to convey a sense of believability, potency, or power to achieve some goal such as intimidating, controlling, or exerting power over others. Some students may want to convey transparency, facetiousness, or a lack of credibility in their threats, where the intention is not to be taken seriously. Nevertheless, the student may privately have either no intention of carrying out the threat, as when threats are intended as "jokes" or pranks, or every intention of carrying out the threat and use minimization and denial to deter efforts at prevention.

Once again, the assessment of a threatener's expectations about how a threat will be perceived by others is complicated by the fact that the student's true intent is difficult to establish. Statements that reflect a wish to lessen fear or concern in others (e.g., "I was just kidding," "Don't take me so seriously") may indeed reflect a wish to clarify that a threat was not accompanied by a genuine intent of harm and was merely expressive or specious. However, statements that are intended to lessen concern may also be meant to deflect attention away from the threatener and to avoid discipline or further questions; yet a clear intention to act violently may still exist once attention from others subsides. Therefore, various hypotheses should be considered about what the threatener wishes to convey in a threatening communication.

What is the victim's perception of the threatener's intent?

If a victim has been identified and the threat has been made directly to the victim, or the victim has been informed of the threat by some third party, it is necessary to obtain some assessment of how serious the victim believes the threat to be. Although victim perceptions can be influenced by anxiety, fear, dislike for the threatener, and similar factors, questioning the targeted victim as to his or her understanding of the seriousness of the threat can often add useful information that can be incorporated into the overall assessment. More specifically, the victim can offer insight into situational triggers that may have provoked the threat, observations on any unusual behaviors that reveal escalating conflicts, inappropriate preoccupation with the victim, and other factors of which the victim may be aware.

If third parties such as other students, teachers, or staff members have learned of the threat, it is also useful to question these individuals and gather information on the circumstances under which the threat was communicated, the threatening student's affect and demeanor when the threat was made, and other behavioral indicators that can provide insight into the psychological state of the student who made the threat. However, one should not be immediately influenced by statements obtained from third parties or victims that suggest a lack of credibility in the threat (e.g., "It was a joke" or "He was just fooling around"). The assessment should include as many individuals as possible who may have information on the context in which the threat was made, with emphasis being given to those who know the threatening student well and who have firsthand knowledge of how, and under what circumstances, the threat was communicated.

Third parties who know the subject should also be interviewed to determine if they have any concerns that the student may act on unusual interests or inappropriate ideas (Fein and Vossekuil, 1998). It is necessary to appraise the motives and interests of these third parties, since parents may minimize or deny evidence of a potential threat because of their desire to protect a child. Likewise, peers may fail to take certain indicators of risk seriously in a student who is viewed as strange or who frequently makes inappropriate comments, and teachers or staff may exaggerate the severity of a threat in students who are perceived as disruptive or who have been stereotyped as troublemakers.

How credible is the threat?

Whether a threat is credible is another key question to ask in the threat assessment process. This leads to the issue of whether a student making a threat is capable of carrying it out, has the means to do so, and intends to commit violence against another person. Credibility is difficult to establish because it depends largely on the private intentions of the person who made the threat (McCann, 1998a). Therefore, credibility, like intent, must be inferred from the content of the threat, the student's behavior, demeanor, emotional state, and the context in which the threat was made.

Several questions should be asked about the credibility of the threat. First, one should focus on the nature of the threatened violence and ask if the student is capable of carrying out the threat. Does the student have access to a weapon? Has a clear plan been formulated? Is it physically possible for the student to carry out the threat? Threats associated with physical assault (e.g., fighting) involve no weapons or special planning and therefore imply that those factors likely to determine if the student becomes violent are situational triggers and provocations. On the other hand, threats associated with using a weapon or detonating a bomb imply a higher degree of planning, and the issue will be whether the student has access to a gun or the materials needed to assemble an explosive device. Establishing credibility of a threat depends on how organized the student is and whether he or she can plan and execute a violent action against the victim (Fein and Vossekuil, 1998).

A second method for exploring credibility is finding out why the student made the threat and what his or her expectations were about how it would impact others. In addition, examine whether the threatening student's story is consistent with his or her actions (Fein and Vossekuil, 1998). For example, a student who writes a short story as a school assignment in which the main character talks about wanting to shoot people, who later says that it was "just a story" and not to be taken seriously, should also be evaluated about associated behaviors. If the student is otherwise well adjusted, does well in school, has a stable family environment, shows no unusual preoccupation with violence, and has no access to weapons, then the evidence points to consistency between the student's explanations and behavior in other areas of his or her life. However, if the student has a history of aggressive acting out in school, serious learning difficulties, poor parental limits and controls, a preoccupation with violence, suicidal thoughts, an unusual interest in guns, and access to a firearm at home, then there is strong evidence that the student's behavior and functioning do not match his or her explanations. In this latter case, the evidence suggests that the student's attempt to make his or her threat appear less credible is intended to deflect attention away from himself or herself.

A third factor related to threat credibility is the presence of planning or of attack-related behaviors that indicate a clear intent to carry out an act of violence. Any evidence that a student is developing a plan of attack, investing energy in targeting specific students (e.g., posting a "hit list" on a Web page), approaching or following someone toward whom the student has an unusual or inappropriate interest (e.g., sending bizarre notes or gifts to classmates), and attempts to avoid detection or evade security measures in the school tend to support the credibility of a threat.

What is the threatener's motive?

It is important to distinguish between three different types of motives when conducting a threat assessment. They include the motive for making a threat, the motive for engaging in attack-related or planning behaviors, and the motive for committing an act of violence. Students can make a threat for any number of reasons, including wanting to influence the behavior of another person, expressing or modulating feelings, instilling fear in others, gaining attention, obtaining a sense of power by disrupting school routines or structure, or raising hope that others will respond and provide some structure or support for which the student cannot otherwise express a need (i.e., "cry for help"). The motivation for engaging in attack-related behaviors (e.g., following the victim, making a "hit list," assembling a bomb, obtaining a weapon) can also be for these as well as other reasons. Students might engage in attack-related behaviors to intimidate others, demonstrate a sense of power and superiority, probe boundaries to test how well security measures work (Mohandie, 2000), and "practice" for a large-scale attack. The motivation for a violent attack is typically a wish to harm the primary target, although other motivations are possible, including gaining attention and notoriety (e.g., media coverage), and suicide, in which the student either plans to kill himself or herself after killing others or hopes to be killed by others during a violent act. In their study of assassins, attackers, and near-lethal approachers, Fein and Vossekuil (1999) found support for three general goals for engaging in lethal or near-lethal violence: harming the target, attention/notoriety, and suicide.

Another factor to evaluate that can provide some insight into the motivation underlying a threatening communication is emotional tone. Although threats are typically viewed as expressions of anger, different forms of hostility must be considered. For instance, some threats may emerge out of frustration, where the student has encountered interference with goal-directed behavior (Folger and Baron, 1996). Frustration is generally conceptualized by social psychologists as the negative emotions associated with individuals being prevented from attaining what they want. Therefore, threats that are made out of frustration may be motivated by situational stressors such as inability to stop other students from teasing, inability to make or keep friends, and inability to repair or reestablish a broken relationship with a boyfriend or girlfriend. Threatening statements can also emerge from hostile attributional biases, in which a person is highly prone to perceive hostile intentions or motives in other people, even when the evidence of anger in other people is equivocal (Folger and Baron, 1996). Some threatening communications may be motivated by anger and hostility resulting from inaccurate perceptions of being the unfair target of hostility from others; these types of threats become a means of self-protection.

Depression may also underlie a threatening communication. Several features of depression, including physiological, emotional, and cognitive symptoms result in diminished functioning across various areas of a person's life. Hopelessness, pessimism, and helplessness may render the person to feel powerless and defenseless. This cognitive pessimism often leads to suicidal ideation and rumination. Threats of violence, when associated with depression and suicidal ideation, should be treated very seriously because hopelessness and pessimism contribute to the perception that violence and suicide are the only means for coping or dealing with a problem or set of difficult circumstances. Moreover, the presence of suicidal ideation or intent indicates that a student has little regard for his or her future and may readily decide to attack others before committing suicide.

The specific content of a threatening statement is also useful for gaining some insight into the motivation and psychological state of the threatening student. Broad statements of threatened violence that fail to identify a specific victim (e.g., "Everyone is going to be sorry," "People will pay") may reflect an expression of intense emotion or may reveal that the threatener is thinking about, but has not yet fully developed, a plan for violence. Threats that target a specific victim or that involve definitive language or behavior (e.g., developing a personal "hit list," "I am going to . . . ") tend to reflect deliberate planning and intent. Therefore, careful analysis of the language used in the threatening communication provides useful information about the intent and motivation of the person making the threat.

Is a secondary gain associated with the threat?

Although threats have a principle motivation, it is also important to consider the presence of any secondary gain, which refers to positive reinforcement that maintains an otherwise maladaptive form of behavior. For example, when children or adolescents engage in delinquent behavior, the attention they receive from peers can reinforce the acting out and increase the likelihood that it will continue, despite any punishment that follows. Threatening communications should also be evaluated with respect to factors that may reinforce the student making a threat. Specific types of secondary gain that should be considered include attention from others, fear or respect from classmates, media attention, and feelings of power or control. Intrinsic factors may reinforce the making of a threat, such as the personality characteristics of the threatener. For example, some students with narcissistic personality traits readily gain a sense of power and control over school officials when their threats cause disruption in the school routine or when repetitive threatening behaviors seem to exasperate administrators. In other cases, the making of threats can be reinforced by a need for approval and acceptance from peers. Therefore, a student with marginal social skills who wishes to be accepted by peers may make a threatening statement or engage in threatening behavior to gain acceptance from the peer group.

Secondary gain should be evaluated as part of the threat assessment process as it can provide insight into the personality factors influencing the making of a threat, as well as the seriousness of a threat. When secondary gain is associated with narcissistic or antisocial traits, such as the need for power, control, or attention, then less focus is placed on the interests of others and the risk for violence is somewhat greater. When secondary gain is associated with inhibited or dependent personality traits, such as the need for social approval, there may be greater sensitivity to the needs of others, which mitigates the risk for violence.

EVALUATING SPECIFIC ISSUES

In addition to direct questions that can be asked about threatening communications, several issues associated with the risk for violence should be examined, including the student's access to weapons, history of violent behavior, psychosocial and environmental stressors that can contribute to violence, group affiliations, and substance abuse.

Weapons

According to data from national surveys of violence in schools, weapon-carrying behavior is more frequent among males than females. Kingery, Coggeshall, and Alford (1998) reviewed results from four anonymous surveys of student attitudes and perceptions on school violence; the use of anonymous surveys was believed to increase the likelihood that students would be more truthful in their self-reports. Results from this research revealed that from 5.9 to 11 percent of males and 1.4 to 4.5 percent of females reported carrying a weapon to school within the previous thirty days. Kingery and his colleagues interpreted these statistics as indicating very high levels of gun-carrying behavior among students in light of the seriousness of bringing a weapon to school. Furthermore, several factors were associated with an increased likelihood of carrying a weapon to school, including having engaged in other violent acts in the past, having carried a gun elsewhere, having pulled a knife or gun on someone within the past year, having used a knife or gun to obtain something from someone in the last year, and having shot or stabbed someone within the last year.

Students who bring a weapon to school are more likely to have been victims of violence. Weapon-carrying students are more likely to have had someone else pull a knife or gun on them, to have been threatened with a weapon either at school or elsewhere, to have been injured by a weapon, to have seen someone else get shot or stabbed, or to have been shot themselves within the last year (Kingery, Coggeshall, and Alford, 1998). Furthermore, the risk for carrying a weapon to school is greater for those students who have engaged in other forms of violent or criminal behavior, including fighting, robbery, gang activity, and selling drugs. Overall, students who bring a weapon to school are involved in a variety of aggressive, violent, and criminal behavior, both as perpetrator and victim.

A weapons assessment is an important part of the evaluation of a student who is believed to pose a threat of violence to others. This assessment should include questions about whether the student or someone in the student's family owns a weapon, including guns, knives, or explosive devices. It is also important to explore other possible avenues through which a student might obtain a weapon, including from friends, fellow gang members, adult friends, and friends of family members.

According to a national survey on patterns of firearms storage in homes in the United States, 35 percent of children under the age of eighteen live in a home where there is at least one firearm present (Schuster et al., 2000). In homes that have both children and firearms, 43 percent had at least one firearm that was stored unlocked, 9 percent had firearms that were unlocked and loaded, and 4 percent had firearms that were unlocked, unloaded, and stored along with ammunition. These findings reveal that in 13 percent of homes where both children and firearms are present, guns are stored in such a way that they are easily accessible to children.

Miller and Hemenway (1999) recommend that the assessment of access to guns address the following basic questions: (1) Is the gun stored loaded or unloaded? (2) Is the gun stored in a locked or unlocked cabinet? (3) Is the ammunition stored locked or unlocked? (4) Are the gun and ammunition stored together or separately? and (5) Is the gun stored assembled or disassembled? These questions will provide the examiner with information needed to determine how accessible a gun is to the child or adolescent, as well as the availability of ammunition.

When asking direct questions about access to weapons, evaluators must also question the student carefully about indirect risk factors associated with carrying a weapon to school. These risk factors include whether the student has ever used a weapon outside of school, and if so under what circumstances. Additional questions should include whether the student has ever (1) been the victim of a crime involving a weapon; (2) been threatened with a weapon outside of school; (3) engaged in violent or aggressive behavior (e.g., fighting) either inside or outside of school; and (4) engaged in high-risk criminal behavior (e.g., gang activity, drug selling). It is important to remember that the presence of any of these factors does not predict that a student will bring a weapon to school, and broad conclusions or generalizations from the information obtained from such an assessment should not be used by itself when making administrative decisions about disposition for the student. A comprehensive weapons assessment should be one piece of the overall evaluation process.

History of Violence

One of the strongest correlates of violent behavior is a history of violence. Aside from being critical to assessing an individual's potential for violence, prior episodes in which the person engaged in aggressive or violent behavior are also informative about the circumstances, stressors, and situations that may provoke a person to become violent. When evaluating a threat or potential threat by a student, as much information as possible should be obtained about prior instances in which the student acted in an aggressive or violent manner and the circumstances under which they occurred.

When interviewing either the student, his or her parents, or other collateral sources who can provide relevant information, direct questions that ask whether the student has been violent can be interpreted in a number of ways and leave open the opportunity for distorted or biased reporting. Asking a student, "Have you ever done anything violent before?" is a close-ended question that calls for a direct "Yes" or "No" response in which the student can deflect further follow-up questioning by simply answering, "No." When asking about a history of violence, it is more useful to ask open-ended questions that presume some level of violent behavior in the past. An alternative way of obtaining information about prior violence is to ask, "What is the most violent thing you have ever done in your life?" This question calls for an open-ended explanation and presumes some level of violence. Responses that are evasive (e.g., "I don't know") can be set aside, and the person can be pressed to provide some response that can be followed up further. Likewise, parents and other collateral sources should be asked open-ended questions, such as "What is the most violent or aggressive thing that . . . has done that you either saw or heard about?"

Once this initial question about the person's history of violence is asked, additional questions should be asked about other incidents that involve aggressive or violent acting out against others. These questions may address episodes of provoked or unprovoked violence, and/or a history of physical fights, assaults, and other forms of interpersonal violence. Follow-up questions should elicit the circumstances under which prior episodes of violence occurred, the stressors that provoked the student's response, verbal statements that accompanied any violent behavior, victim characteristics and relationship to the student, whether a weapon was used, and other related factors. Careful attention should also be paid to the amount of planning, or lack thereof, that went into a violent act and the organization of the person's behavior following the incident.

The student's history of arrests or other legal difficulties should also be evaluated to determine the extent to which they were associated with violence or aggression. It may be necessary to identify not only those prior criminal acts that are associated with violence toward other people but also those associated with violence against property. The circumstances surrounding property crimes, such as vandalism and burglary, should be fully explored regarding the student's motivation. For instance, some forms of vandalism are motivated by group behavior that does not target a specific individual, while other property crimes are motivated by resentment or a need for revenge against a specific person or group of persons. It is also important to look for evidence in property crimes that suggests hate group activity or the condoning of violence against certain groups of people, which indicates a more organized intent to inflict harm on others. In addition, some burglaries committed by adolescents are committed under bizarre circumstances or are sexually motivated by fetishes or voyeurism (McCann, 2000a). Sexually motivated burglaries are suggestive of an increased risk for escalating sexual violence and should be considered indicative of a need for more intensive assessment and treatment for the offending student. Therefore, it is important to assess not only episodes of violent criminal activity that target other people but also nonviolent crimes involving destruction of property, burglary, and vandalism.

When evaluating a student's history of violent behavior, one should look for symptoms of mental illness that may be associated with violence. More specifically, questions should be directed at determining whether the student's behavior was influenced by command auditory hallucinations, delusions, paranoid beliefs, depression or severe hopelessness, or intense anxiety. In addition, the assessment should focus on any unusual beliefs, behaviors, or preoccupations, such as stalking, inappropriate interest in violence (e.g., assassination, serial killers), or radical ideas and beliefs. The co-occurrence of violent behavior and serious mental illness or bizarre behavior suggests that the student has periods of impaired judgment, insight, or reality testing that can precipitate aggressive or violent acting out.

Psychosocial History

A complete psychosocial history should be obtained on a student who makes or poses a threat of violence; useful information can be obtained not only on factors related to an increased risk for violence but also on factors that may inhibit or reduce risk. Information should be collected about the student's family history, including parents, siblings, stability of family relationships, history of parental divorce or separation, and other information on the cohesiveness of the student's family environment. In addition, detailed information should be obtained about the student's educational history, including schools attended, level of academic achievement, history of disciplinary problems, repeated grades, and whether special educational services have ever been needed.

Information about a student's extracurricular activities, including interests, hobbies, and involvement with organizations, can also be useful for identifying skills that provide feelings of competency and self-efficacy for the student. A lack of involvement in activities or hobbies, or an excessive investment in solitary or asocial activities (e.g., computer chat rooms) denotes social isolation that can exacerbate feelings of estrangement and isolation. Social detachment can reflect a lack of social support, sensitivity to rejection, or a lack of interpersonal sensitivity or empathy that can be useful for appraising a student's relative risk for violence.

Social Environment

Several aspects of a student's social environment are relevant to threat assessment. A student's social environment can be broadly defined to encompass all those social factors that impact on his or her behavior.

Peer relationships in later childhood and adolescence are extremely important for emotional and psychological development and exert considerable influence over a student's behavior. When children first begin school, they begin to explore relationships with other people outside the immediate family. As the child enters adolescence, peers begin to replace parents or primary caregivers as important figures in the young person's life. Therefore, it is important to question the subject of a threat assessment about peer relationships, including who are considered "best friends," the kinds of activities that are done with peers, attitudes and beliefs that peers have about various matters, and sources of peer rejection or teasing, if any. Information about peer relationships can be obtained in an unobtrusive manner. One method is to ask the student what kinds of things he or she likes to do with friends and how friends have reacted to the student's behavior at various times. If the focus of the assessment is on a threatening communication, it is often instructive to ask the student if friends are aware that the threat was made and how they reacted to it if they are aware. This approach allows the examiner to determine if the student's peers endorse threatening or violent behavior as a means of coping with problems, as well as whether peers have taken the student's threat seriously. In turn, the student's feelings about how peers have reacted can be explored.

Bonding to school is another factor that has been identified as a risk factor for violence among children and adolescents. In particular, this refers to a child or adolescent's feelings of connectedness and attachment to the academic setting. Several factors provide some measure of school bonding and should be considered when assessing whether a student poses a threat. Grades are one index of school performance and may indirectly reflect the degree of attachment a student has to school; they can be examined both formally through school records and through the student's self-reports. The student's feelings of confidence and adequacy about school can also be gauged during the interview. Another index of school bonding is the number of schools a student has attended; again, this can be determined through collateral or self-reports and from school records. If the student has attended several elementary schools, this may reflect disruption in the child or adolescent's attachments to peers and school, as well as disruptive changes in family residences or the parents' marriage.

Information should also be obtained about any hospitalizations the student has had, including not only those for psychiatric reasons but also medical problems. By obtaining information on dates, the circumstances under which hospitalizations occurred, and the reasons for admission, the threat assessment team can evaluate how much disruption these hospitalizations have caused in the student's life, the effectiveness of treatment, and the presence of any medical or psychiatric conditions that may bear on the student's potential for violence.

Group Affiliations

Several factors related to a student's involvement with or membership in a peer or social group should be examined. The various concerns include whether the youth is a gang member, associates with peers with violent or counterculture attitudes, or socializes with others who endorse violent or aggressive attitudes. According to Reddy Pynchon and Borum (1999), several social psychological issues are useful for understanding and evaluating the impact of group membership on an individual's behavior. For instance, research from social psychology has demonstrated that personal opinions and attitudes become more extreme in the context of a group; a person's style of solving problems can become more distorted or faulty due to group pressures; and members of groups are viewed more positively by the group and nonmembers are viewed less favorably. Perhaps most important is the fact that group membership permits a diffusion of responsibility in which an individual can feel less responsible for an act of violence by passing accountability on to other group members (Reddy Pynchon and Borum, 1999).

When evaluating group influences in school settings, a number of factors should be considered. According to Reddy Pynchon and Borum (1999), key questions that should be asked with respect to the type of group involved include the following: (1) What are the norms of the group? (2) What is the structure of the group? (3) How cohesive is the group? and (4) What is the group's current situation? It is very helpful for school officials, mental health professionals, and other individuals who must evaluate school-based threats to be familiar with current trends in popular culture, including slang expressions, fashion, music, and media. Also, familiarity with social groupings within the school and community is helpful for identifying students who associate with one another. These factors will assist in identifying the leaders, norms for various peer groups, and how cohesive various groups are within a specific school or community.

Another means of evaluating group affiliations in school settings is exploring the effect of group membership on individual behavior. For instance, the benefits and costs of group membership influence whether a student will seek out and be influenced by others outside the group. Students who are considered outsiders can lose or gain personal status as a result of their rejection or acceptance by a particular social group. For example, the social rewards of approval and heightened status are greater for a student who is both a popular athlete and high academic achiever if the student avoids associating with bright students who are nevertheless looked down upon by others because they are socially inept. In short, it is important to appraise the various rewards and costs of group membership. Certain groups have expectations of the degree of conformity that is demanded of individual members. It is often necessary to become familiar with the rules of compliance and obedience and to learn the consequences of defiance. For example, many gangs have rituals in which new members must participate; moreover, deviation from gang norms can result in aggressive responses from other gang members. The more severe the consequences for defying group norms, the more likely that individual members will be influenced by and comply with the demands of other group members.

Finally, Reddy Pynchon and Borum (1999) suggest questions be asked about how a person may be affected by group membership. When assessing the impact of peer groups on student behavior, the following questions should be raised: (1) How important is the peer or social group to the student? (2) What personal factors increase or reduce the likelihood that the student will deviate from the group norms? and (3) What is the individual student's propensity to be induced by the group to engage in violent or extreme behavior?

An issue related to group membership is the youth's religious belief system. Information on the student's religious affiliations and beliefs can be very useful in some cases for evaluating factors that exacerbate or inhibit the propensity for violence. A student's strong religious beliefs, which are important to him or her and which are similar to those of close family members, may serve as an inhibiting factor due to the incompatibility the student may feel between these beliefs and violent behavior. On the other hand, some adolescents are drawn to fringe religious groups or atypical practices (e.g., satanic interests, the occult) that may contribute to aggressive behavior. In addition, some students may be experiencing symptoms of psychosis, such as hallucinations or delusions, that have a religious content. These should be fully evaluated.

Biological Factors

It is important to have information on medical conditions or symptoms and a history of physical injuries that may impact on the student's propensity for violence. Relevant issues include whether the student has a history of neurological problems that influence his or her behavior, including closed head injuries, seizure disorders, and neurological disorders. Although some neurological difficulties have little impact on the student's potential for violence, others (e.g., closed head injury with frontal lobe damage) can increase the risk for violent and aggressive behavior. Therefore, consultation with a neurologist or other medical specialist who can provide input on the behavioral manifestations of certain medical conditions may be needed in some cases.

The assessment should also yield as much information as possible on the developmental history of the student, including the mother's pregnancy and delivery. Any complications (e.g., oxygen deprivation) or adverse environmental conditions (e.g., maternal alcohol or drug use during pregnancy) should also be noted. It may be necessary to obtain input from the school physician, the student's pediatrician, or some other qualified medical professional on any medications the student is currently taking, and information should also be obtained about potential side effects. If the student is taking psychotropic medications, the reasons for the medications being prescribed and their treatment effects, or lack thereof, should be noted in the record.

Substance Abuse

The presence of substance abuse raises the risk for violence. Aside from the general question of whether a student is abusing substances, questions should be asked related to the types of substances being used and their effects on the student's behavior. Alcohol abuse can increase the potential for aggression because of its disinhibiting effects, while other drugs have different behavioral effects. Psychostimulants, such as amphetamines and cocaine, can result in states of extreme euphoria, psychomotor agitation, and grandiose or paranoid thinking that can provoke violent outbursts (Meloy, 2000). Other substances, such as marijuana and hallucinogenic agents, can result in impaired judgment and acute paranoid thinking that markedly impair coping mechanisms that may otherwise protect against aggressive episodes.

The assessment of substance abuse should be directed at several issues associated with the use of alcohol or drugs, including not only the types of substances used, but also frequency of use, the length of time that the youth has used substances, circumstances under which substances are ingested, and psychological and behavioral effects. Evidence of possible psychological or physical dependence should also be examined, including signs of tolerance (i.e., increasing amounts of the substance ingested to achieve similar effects), loss of control over use (i.e., binges, blackouts), and withdrawal (i.e., physiological symptoms when the substance is no longer available). The presence of substance dependence should alert the examiner to a more significant problem that requires intensive treatment.

A major problem is the issue of denial and minimization that occurs when people who use alcohol or drugs excessively are asked about their patterns of use. Although it is necessary to ask direct questions about how much alcohol and what drugs the student uses, one must also develop indirect patterns of questioning that will circumvent direct denials. Collateral information should be sought from others who know the student and who can provide information about suspected substance abuse. In addition, many adolescents may be willing to admit occasional substance use, while minimizing frequency or amount of use. Therefore, additional questions should probe collateral evidence of potential substance abuse problems, such as negative comments from others (e.g., parents, girlfriend, boyfriend), job loss related to drug use, acute intoxication requiring medical attention (i.e., accidental overdoses), blackouts, legal difficulties, and distorted beliefs about substance use (e.g., one must use alcohol or drugs at a party to fit in socially or have a good time).

INDIRECT METHODS OF ASSESSMENT

A major challenge faced by professionals who evaluate a student who has made a threat is differentiating between students who pose a threat and those who do not. The problem in school cases, however, is that students may engage in pre-attack behavior that is observed by others who cannot appraise the seriousness of the behavior (e.g., peers) or who may endorse the intended violence (e.g., fellow gang members, peers who support violence). In some cases, the threatener's intentions cannot be evaluated until after the fact because they were never communicated to another person or they were documented in ways that preclude timely discovery (e.g., diaries). The assessment of threats must often rely on indirect methods that focus on behavioral indicators and patterns that are suggestive, but not definitive predictors of an increased risk for violence. Indirect signs of violence potential must be interpreted cautiously and should not be used to profile students or target students whose mildly aggravating behavior creates management difficulties in the school setting.

Verbal Indicators

Verbal behavior can sometimes provide indirect, yet valuable, information on a person's potential for violence. Statements revealing personal loss, emotional distress (e.g., anger, depression, anxiety), and general verbal hostility are often associated with behavioral instability and a propensity for violence. Therefore, recent suicidal threats or comments denote the onset of hopelessness in which a student has less concern for the consequences of his or her actions. The use of profanity, verbal insults, and intimidating statements can also be used to make inferences about a student's emotional state. If verbal aggression becomes more frequent and represents a change from the student's normal level of functioning, or if verbal aggression is chronic and accompanied by other acting-out behaviors, then the student may need to be referred for mental health assessment and treatment, increased monitoring (e.g., more frequent sessions with a guidance counselor or therapist), or special education programs.

Other verbal indicators of violence potential include suicidal threats, gestures, or statements that reflect feelings of hopelessness or pessimism about life. The co-occurrence of threats of violence and suicide points to a potentially dangerous situation because there are few psychological factors inhibiting impulses or intentions. If a student is considering an act of violence while also considering suicide, he or she is less likely to be dissuaded by negative consequences or punishment. The potentially violent and suicidal student is more susceptible to feeling as though other victims should join him or her in death, and feelings of hopelessness and pessimism increase the chances that the adolescent will not care about what happens as a result of his or her actions. Verlinden, Hersen, and Thomas (2000) found that many school assailants experienced feelings of depression and made suicidal threats prior to school shooting incidents. Therefore, verbal statements involving themes of both violence and suicide or self-destruction should be taken as strong evidence of a heightened risk for violence in cases where the student has made or poses a threat to others.

The conversations and verbal statements of some students may be dominated by negative themes that raise concerns about the student's emotional state or behavioral propensities. More specifically, some students show intolerance of others, prejudice or hatred toward minorities or members of certain groups, and excessive preoccupations with violence. Although such verbal statements tend to indicate intolerance and a lack of empathy for others, they should not necessarily justify targeting a student as potentially violent or a threat to others. Rather, verbal communications of intolerance or hatred should be addressed more generally by the school administration as behavior that is not conducive to student education. Interventions or responses, such as behavioral discipline or referral for psychological assessment and treatment, can be predicated on the nature of the verbal messages, rather than as a means of singling out certain students when no other indicators of violence potential have been identified.

Nonverbal Indicators

Well-controlled studies on school violence are difficult to conduct because ethical and practical constraints preclude researchers from randomly assigning students to experimental conditions or exposing them to potentially violent circumstances. Moreover, the low base rate of school violence in general makes it difficult to collect data on large numbers of violent incidents. In addition, threatening behavior among students has only recently become a focus of attention and thus empirical research on student threats is limited.

A key nonverbal factor that has been observed in most cases of lethal school violence is a recent loss that was experienced by the youth prior to the violent episode. McGee and DeBernardo (1999) found in a sample of thirteen students who shot and either killed or seriously wounded someone in a school setting that most were exposed to multiple psychological stressors involving real or imagined loss, abandonment, rejection, or loss of status or esteem as a result of censure or discipline. Likewise, Verlinden, Hersen, and Thomas (2000) found that most school assailants in their sample experienced some significant loss, such as a breakup with a girlfriend, loss of status or esteem due to excessive teasing, or some other rejection or perceived abandonment prior to a school shooting. These findings are consistent with those of Fein and Vossekuil (1999) in their study of individuals who assassinated, or approached with lethal means, a public figure. In each of these studies, a triggering event associated with loss of some significant status (e.g., job) or relationship, or another form of rejection preceded an act of lethal or near-lethal violence. Therefore, students suffering personal loss, rejection, abandonment, or loss of status should be given high priority for further assessment and monitoring.

Some nonverbal behaviors that should be carefully evaluated involve *boundary probing,* which occurs when a student recognizes certain limits or social boundaries and tests them to see if they can be violated (Mohandie, 2000). An example of boundary probing occurs when a student brings a weapon to school without any intention of committing an act of violence. Given the considerable attention and publicity that has been given to school violence and the measures that have been taken to increase safety in many schools (e.g., installation of video surveillance equipment, posting of security officers at entrances), students are well aware of rules and policies that have been implemented. Consequently, some adolescents with oppositional tendencies who like to challenge authority may engage in boundary probing to test the response of school officials when certain rules are violated. However, some boundary probing leads to increasingly more threatening and potentially violent action. For example, if two students have an ongoing conflict requiring school officials to set limits (e.g., warnings, suspensions), these limits may be violated as each student seeks to intimidate or challenge the other.

It is often difficult to discern between students who probe boundaries with the intent merely to challenge authority and students who are violence prone and probe boundaries in preparation for a calculated plan of attack. Therefore, repetitive rule violations, major rule violations (e.g., bringing a concealed weapon to school), and violations of school policies and rules that show a pattern of increasing severity should be considered boundary probing that would require more extensive assessment and immediate intervention.

Media Influences

Debates over whether violence in the media, including video games and movies, is a cause of violent behavior in young people seem to frame the relationship between violence and the media inappropriately. The existence of numerous children and adolescents who are exposed to violence in the media and who do not end up becoming violent falsifies the notion that media violence is a definitive cause of violence in young people. However, it is clear in many cases of school violence that assailants have shown an unusual preoccupation with violent themes in the media. Although some relationship exists between violence and the media, it is not clearly understood. A useful analogy for violence in the media and its link to juvenile violence is the elements of a fire. Three elements are required for a fire to ignite: heat, fuel, and oxygen. If any one of these three components is removed, a fire cannot burn. Although heat, often in the form of a spark or lighted match, is generally viewed as the "cause" of a fire, combustion cannot occur without fuel and oxygen, which are necessary but not sufficient components of a fire. Violence in the media can be viewed similarly as one form of fuel that contributes to violence; however, it is not the only component, and it is not a fueling agent in every case. Certain children and adolescents who are predisposed to act violently, through a combination of psychological, situational, social, and other factors, are more prone to act in a violent manner when they are regularly exposed to violent video games, television program, or movies. In short, violence in the media may best be conceptualized as a catalyst or facilitating agent for violent behavior in some students who are predisposed, rather than a major causal factor.

As part of a threat assessment protocol, the interests a student has in television programs, movies, computer and video games, and other media influences should be explored. More specifically, the student should be asked about television shows that are watched regularly, including the amount of time spent watching television, with whom the student watches, and the reasons particular shows are of interest. All of these factors provide information on the viewing patterns of the student. Those students who watch programs with violent content, and who do so alone, should be probed further to explore how they deal with fantasies or thoughts that are prompted by themes or images that are encountered. If the youth watches television programs with friends or peers, then it is likewise useful to explore how violent themes are discussed with friends, including whether the use of violence is endorsed by peers as an acceptable outlet for aggressive feelings. If the youth watches television programs with siblings or parents, then one should also explore the manner in which violent themes are treated, including whether older siblings encourage the expression of violence, younger siblings are potential victims of violence, and whether parents monitor the youth's exposure to violent television programs.

Other media influences, including movie interests, video games, and computer habits can also be assessed. One should explore whether parents monitor or restrict the youth's access to violent movies through supervision or by restricting access to movies that are rated for violence.

A useful source of information on the student's media influences is asking about his or her computer habits. Students often have access to Web sites, bulletin boards, and mailing lists that provide information on violence (e.g., bomb making), opportunities to correspond with others who endorse the use of violence as a means of solving problems (e.g., chat rooms), and information the student may have posted that reflects thoughts or feelings about potential targets. One method of assessing or evaluating a student's personal beliefs is to ask during the course of the interview if the student has computer access and a personal Web page. If so, then asking for the Internet address and independently reviewing the student's page may yield useful information about unusual interests or inappropriate messages. Also, one can ask the student if he or she has a list of frequently visited or bookmarked Web sites and, if so, to provide the examiner with the names and Internet addresses of these sites. Other information may include bulletin boards that the student utilizes and mailing lists to which he or she belongs.

ASSESSING POTENTIAL INHIBITORS OF VIOLENCE

Although a considerable amount of focus has been placed on factors associated with an increased risk for violence, those conducting a threat assessment should not overlook factors that may inhibit or reduce the potential for violence. Research on risk assessment in children and adolescents is rather scant (Grisso, 1998) and that which has been conducted has focused on identifying factors associated with increased risk for violence. The identification of personal stabilizing factors that can diminish the potential for violence must proceed rationally and intuitively. For instance, a history of violent behavior may be a strong predictor of future violence, but this is an unchangeable factor. On the other hand, the potential for violence can be reduced by changing environmental factors, such as reducing crowding and making room temperatures more comfortable.

Kinney (1996) has identified a number of potential inhibitors to violence in the workplace that can be adapted and applied in the school setting. Among the factors he identified were: a secure and stable family life; rational and future-oriented thinking; a lack of drug or alcohol use; emotional stability; community ties and supports; having outside interests and hobbies; supportive friendships; a lack of criminal personality propensities; and religious involvement. Consequently, factors that are likely to inhibit violent acting out among students include: supportive family relationships; parental support and structure; a sense of hope; good judgment; absence of drug or alcohol use;

emotional stability; strong ties to prosocial community organizations (e.g., sports); outside interests and hobbies (e.g., music); supportive friendships with peers who have prosocial attitudes; no propensity toward delinquency or psychopathy; strong attachment and bonding to school; and religious or spiritual commitments.

Some of these factors can be used in developing interventions for students who have threatened or who may pose a threat to others. For example, if a student has an important social relationship with a peer who does not condone violence as a means of resolving conflict and who can provide support to the student, this relationship should be developed as an anchoring point for the student. Likewise, if a student has an area where he or she has some degree of personal competence (e.g., music, sports), then this can be encouraged and supported. It is important to recognize that inhibiting factors and anchoring points in a student's life should not be assessed and weighed in a rigid fashion, since some factors may be more important than others. A student may have several inhibiting factors present that suggest a relatively low level of risk; however, if these anchors are associated with one or two very strong risk-enhancing factors (e.g., an organized plan of violence that the student intends to carry out at a specific time and place), then the evaluation must weigh these latter factors more heavily.

INTERDISCIPLINARY APPROACHES

The process of assessing and managing student threats should not be assigned to a specific individual; rather, threat assessment should be performed by a team of professionals each of whom represent different disciplines and contribute their unique expertise (Hinman and Cook, 2001; Mohandie, 2000). Evaluating threatening communications and situations in a school setting may involve input from school administrators, psychologists, guidance counselors, social workers, and teachers; in some cases, security or law enforcement officers may be required. The exact composition of a threat assessment and management team will depend on several factors, including staffing patterns, the availability of financial resources for hiring outside consultants, and the school district's level of commitment to establishing a threat assessment and management program.

In some cases, additional consultation or input may be needed depending on the results of the initial assessment or the particular nature of the threatening communication. Input from a physician or school nurse may be indicated in those cases where the identified student has a medical condition or is taking medication that may affect his or her behavior. Other types of specialized input from experts may be needed. Examples include an expert on satanic cults where a student or group of students is engaging in satanic rituals; someone knowledgeable in the customs and norms of other cultures when the identified student is from a culture different from that of the United States; and computer experts who can help trace the origin of anonymous electronic threats made on computers within the school (Hinman and Cook, 2001). Although different types of input might be needed, much will depend on the specific facts and dynamics of the individual case.

CONCLUSION

The identification and assessment of threatening communications or situations involving students is a process that is complicated by the fact that definitive prediction of violent behavior is not possible. Moreover, the use of profiling techniques to identify students who may pose a threat of violence is controversial because it may inappropriately target some students as dangerous. The assessment of threatening communications and situations must encompass many levels of inquiry directed at different aspects of the student's behavior and personal history. If a direct threat is made, then appraisal of several factors is necessary, including the student's intent, clarity in making the threat, motivation, and credibility. Other factors should also be assessed, including the student's access to weapons, prior history of violence, social environment, patterns of substance abuse, and overall level of functioning. When a student poses, but has not made, a direct threat to others, there are greater challenges to making an effective assessment. Although indirect methods of assessment are recommended, including evaluation of verbal and nonverbal indicators, media influences, and factors that tend to inhibit a student's potential for violence, this type of data must be used cautiously and not as behavioral or profile indicators that inappropriately target certain students. Rather, less direct forms of information should focus on behavior and patterns of conduct, with interventions planned to maximize the student's adaptation and adjustment. The next chapter outlines the close relationship between threat assessment and management.

Chapter 5

Managing Potentially Violent Situations

The management of student threats is closely tied to the assessment process. Rather than two separate phases of dealing with potentially violent situations, assessment and management comprise a dynamic process in which each informs the other, resulting in a system that guides case management. Assessment of a threat and the risk factors associated with a potential for violence should lead to the identification of interventions and case management strategies that will hopefully reduce risk. Similarly, the success of various interventions must be assessed to determine if they work. This reassessment process, in turn, leads to modification of the interventions selected. Therefore, a process develops in which risk factors are identified, interventions implemented, the effectiveness of interventions assessed, modifications undertaken, and a reassessment made of the effectiveness of these newer interventions. The process of assessment does not end once relevant risk-enhancing and risk-inhibiting factors have been identified. Assessment is part of the case management of student threats, and periodic assessments are indicated until the student is no longer deemed to be a risk to others. The relationship between assessment and intervention can be compared to a feedback loop, as represented in Figure 5.1.

In the same way that a student's potential for violence can be classified according to relative degrees of risk, interventions and case management strategies can range in their degree of intensity and structure. More specifically, interventions can be arranged hierarchically in terms of the frequency with which they are made (i.e., dosage), their level of intrusiveness, the degree of disruption they create in school procedures, and the specific area of the person's life that they target (e.g., psychological, social). Some interventions are relatively benign and unintrusive, such as behavioral monitoring, whereas others call for moderate disruptions in a student's life, such as referral

FIGURE 5.1. Interactive Relationship Between Assessment and Intervention

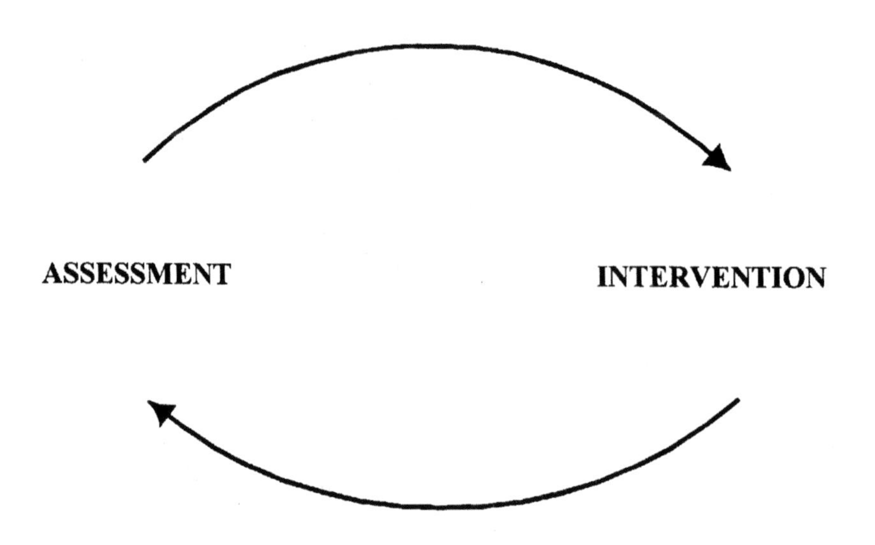

for mental health treatment or suspension from school. The most intrusive and restrictive interventions include expulsion from school, involuntary hospitalization, and arrest.

Violence is a process that is dependent on several factors, therefore it follows that interventions must also be multifaceted and arranged so that they address different risk factors. Violence is a contextual behavior that arises out of a complex interaction of the perpetrator's individual characteristics, the victim's individual characteristics, and situational variables that relate to stressors and triggers that impact on the interaction between perpetrator and victim.

Sometimes several interventions can be implemented at the same time, such as when a student with a serious mental illness who has access to a gun in the home and has made a threat against another student requires inpatient hospitalization. In addition to involuntary civil commitment, this situation also requires removal of all weapons from the home and possibly notification of the potential victim. In other situations, multiple interventions may be taken sequentially, such as in the case of a student with attention deficit hyperactivity disorder who has exhibited a pattern of increasingly more aggressive behavior in school. The primary focus of intervention may be on treating the student's attention deficit hyperactivity disorder with medication and behavioral psychotherapy, followed by an assessment of the student's adjustment in school. If the aggression continues, then more restrictive interventions may need to take place, such as home schooling or alternative educational placement.

In this chapter, specific case management strategies are outlined with respect to potentially violent students, victims, and situational factors. These interventions are separated into four broad categories: behavioral, social and environmental, psychological, and legal. Although the goal of threat assessment and management is to prevent future acts of violence and aggression, a violent act in a school has an adverse psychological impact on other students. In these cases, interventions must turn to helping students deal with the potentially traumatic impact that violence has on victims and survivors. Therefore, a comprehensive approach to dealing with the psychological aftermath of school violence, known as critical incident stress management, will be briefly outlined.

INTERVENTIONS TARGETING THE POTENTIALLY VIOLENT STUDENT

Behavioral Interventions

Behavioral psychologists and therapists have long recognized that behavior sometimes undergoes changes in frequency or intensity when it is merely being observed or monitored. In younger children, this tends to occur when the child knows that a parent, teacher, or some other important adult is watching. If the child is playing a sport, extra effort may be given to earn praise, or the child may be more conscientious, follow rules, and show better sportsmanship. In short, children or adolescents will modify their behavior when they know that someone else is watching.

With respect to the management of potentially violent situations, one of the least restrictive measures that can be taken is to monitor a student's behavior. This can occur in any number of ways. Behavioral monitoring may be instituted by having hall monitors observe the student more frequently, maintaining awareness of a student's whereabouts at all times while he or she is in the school building, or having a specific staff member make regular visual contact with the student at various times during the school day. Visual monitoring can be scheduled at any desired time interval, such as hourly, by school period, or daily.

Other forms of behavioral monitoring are more structured and involve direct contact with the student. Regularly scheduled meetings can be arranged with the school guidance counselor, assistant principal, or some other school official. These meetings might involve discussing changes in the student's emotional state and stressors, situational factors that are affecting the student's daily adjustment, or the collection of information that can be used for ongoing assessment and case management. Once again, the frequency and duration of these meetings can be scheduled as needed, including daily, twice a week, or weekly.

Another form of behavioral monitoring that overlaps somewhat with social and environmental interventions is regular family meetings with the student's parents. The initial phases of assessment may include speaking with the parents of the student who has come to the attention of school officials. Although these meetings are valuable for collecting information related to family stressors and disruptions, the presence of violence-promoting attitudes in the home, and similar types of data, they also constitute a useful behavioral monitoring intervention and can be scheduled as needed. The focus of these meetings may be merely gathering information on school assignments, the student's adjustment, and changes in family circumstances. Greater involvement of parents may be helpful in making the student feel supported by family members; likewise, a lack of parental interest in speaking with school officials may reveal problems such as a lack of social support, weak behavioral limits, or oppositional behavior outside the school setting.

It is important to keep the emotional tone of these regular family meetings neutral and nonaccusatory so they do not turn into sessions where the student is berated. The primary focus should be collection of information, monitoring of the student's adjustment, and providing direction and support to parents. If more severe interventions, such as suspension or expulsion, must be implemented, these plans must be conveyed in an objective manner during family meetings.

One ill-advised technique some school officials use to deal with threatening situations is to have joint meetings with the targeted student and potential victim. For example, cases involving a male student with an obsessive preoccupation toward a female student frequently involve stalking or sexually harassing behaviors in which the male student sends inappropriate messages that instill fear in the female student and her parents. In some of these cases, well-meaning school officials or counselors attempt to bring the two students together to work out a compromise where the harassment can stop on "friendly" terms. This intervention should be strongly discouraged and avoided at all costs in school settings; *conjoint meetings between a threatening student and a targeted victim is not a sound intervention strategy*. There are many risks with this type of approach, including encouraging a student's fantasies and obsessive preoccupation with the victim, projection of anger or rage onto the victim for alerting school officials to threats that may have been made, and other adverse emotional consequences (e.g., revenge) brought about by attempting to bring together the identified student and his or her potential victim. Interventions directed at the individual student and victim should be instituted in such a way that contact between the two parties is minimized.

Social and Environmental Interventions

Some procedures for preventing school violence that are directed at the immediate social environment can be applied broadly and do not necessarily target specific students. Many of these procedures involve behavioral monitoring and include such measures as installing video cameras to monitor school grounds, banning all but transparent bookbags, installing metal detectors at entrances, and similar measures aimed at reducing the risk for violence. Although many of these procedures are implemented primarily from a security standpoint and may be effective in some ways, they are not infallible and can be circumvented if a student is very intent on carrying out an act of violence in school. The shooting in Jonesboro, Arkansas, is one such example, in which two students set off a fire alarm and opened fire on students and teachers outside of the school as the building was being evacuated. Such careful planning by some school assailants indicates that security measures within the school must be supplemented with other threat assessment and management strategies.

Social and environmental interventions should supplement but not replace existing security measures within the school. Also, they should not be used as punitive measures for those students who may be targeted as "troublemakers" or who are believed to fit the "profile" of a violent student. Rather, these measures are intended to be used when a specific threat has been made or in situations where a student's behavior and conduct has been identified as posing a serious risk to others.

Among the least restrictive and intrusive social or environmental measures that can be taken to manage a student who is a potential threat is to implement a change in class scheduling. This may merely constitute placing the student in a schedule that is different from that of the identified victim, or it may require reducing as much as possible the contact one student has with another by arranging class schedules so the students do not have any contact with each other during the school day.

More restrictive social and environmental changes may be required in cases in which a student's behavior is volatile, threatening, or difficult to manage. These interventions include in-building suspension, where the student is assigned to a room within the school building for a day and is intensively monitored by a staff member. Out-of-school suspension may also be required if the student's behavior constitutes a major violation of school rules. The most extreme changes to a student's school environment are those involving permanent removal from the school setting through either assignment to home schooling or expulsion. Each of these courses of action, including suspension, home schooling, and expulsion, may have limited impact on a student's behavior. In some cases, suspension or expulsion could be interpreted by the student as a loss of status or rejection that precipitates a motive for revenge against the school or other students who may have reported the student's behavior. Furthermore, these actions do not address underlying psychological and social problems that need to be addressed through other interventions or supportive action. It is important not to view suspension or expulsion as punitive measures for misbehavior; they should be viewed as necessary in those cases where student safety and discipline need to be preserved. Other referrals should be made for psychological treatment to facilitate the student's placement in a setting that maximizes the potential for his or her social adjustment.

Another set of social interventions that may be of help in managing situations where a student has made or poses a threat of harm to others involves mobilization of the student's family. Disruptions in a child or adolescent's family, including the presence of child abuse, parental drug abuse, criminality, and other stressors in the family environment contribute to an increased risk for aggression and violence. In some cases, parents of the student may show little or no interest in working with the school, or they may simply not be available. Nevertheless, some effort should be made to involve parents in the case management process, either by increasing the monitoring of the student's behavior at home, implementing changes in the student's habits and interests outside of school (e.g., limiting access to media with violent themes), and/or limiting access to peers who may provoke or precipitate the student's aggression.

Psychological Interventions

A number of mental health interventions can take place in cases where a student's potential for violence is uncertain or where there is some evidence of psychological disturbance that may require further assessment and treatment. Because referral for mental health treatment is more intrusive than behavioral monitoring and may be met with resistance by the student and his or her parents, it may be challenging to get the student those needed services or programs. Nevertheless, mental health assessment and treatment can be obtained either by directing that the parents of the student obtain an evaluation for the student, providing mental health consultation services through the school, or utilizing school psychologists and social workers who are employed in the school setting.

Referrals for mental health assessment and treatment should be considered when there is evidence of psychological problems that must be evaluated further or that require treatment. Examples of some problems that require this type of approach include: suicidal threats or gestures; severe oppositional and defiant behavior; anxiety; depression; preoccupation with violence; bizarre thinking and preoccupations; recurrent anger; and similar signs of emotional disturbance. Evidence of alcohol or drug abuse should also be evaluated further, and a referral for substance abuse treatment should be made when the student has a problem with excessive drug or alcohol use. Depending on the specific problems a student presents, several treatment approaches may be considered, including anger management, empathy training, family therapy, behavioral management of attentional difficulties, and individual psychotherapy for problems related to low self-image, abuse, or other relevant issues. In addition, varying levels of outpatient mental health care are available for children and adolescents, depending on the severity of their behavioral or psychological disturbances. The least restrictive mental health treatment involves individual, group, or family therapy in an outpatient setting. More restrictive programs may be required for severe levels of disturbance, including (1) an after-school program where the student attends a structured mental health treatment program each day after school; (2) a day treatment program that has both educational and psychological treatment components and that the child or adolescent attends each day but still lives at home; or (3) a residential treatment program where the child or adolescent resides in a structured living setting that includes comprehensive educational, social, and psychological treatment programs.

Among the most intrusive and restrictive of mental health interventions is involuntary hospitalization for students who present an imminent risk of harm to either themselves or others. The decision to admit a child or adolescent to an inpatient psychiatric facility typically occurs after evaluation by psychiatric emergency room personnel, including a physician. In those situations where a child or adolescent is exhibiting disorganized, extremely volatile, or imminently violent behavior, he or she will need to go to a hospital for evaluation, transported by parents or law enforcement officers, depending on the degree of volatility in the student's behavior.

In some cases where a student is treated in an outpatient setting, a referral for psychiatric consultation may be indicated if the student presents with severe symptoms that will benefit from psychotropic medication. Specific problems that indicate a need for medical consultation include symptoms of attention deficit hyperactivity disorder, disturbances in thinking, delusions, hallucinations, severe depression, and marked anxiety. Medication should be viewed as an adjunct to, not a replacement for, other forms of psychological treatment that involve frequent and regular therapeutic contact with the student, such as individual or family psychotherapy.

A major component of the mental health services that are offered to students who have made or pose a threat to others is risk assessment of violent behavior. Violence risk assessment involves careful analysis of the psychological, situational, and psychosocial history, and clinical factors that may enhance or inhibit the potential for violence. These factors were outlined previously; however, it is important to recognize that violence risk assessment is not a static, one-time decision about a student's propensity for violence. Rather, periodic risk assessment is needed when situational variables change, stressors become more or less intense, or the student experiences changes in his or her psychological functioning. Therefore, consideration should be given to the number, frequency, and timing of periodic risk assessments as the situation or case demands.

Psychoeducational assessment of students is very familiar activity to school psychologists, special education teachers, and other professionals who are in a position to make sure that students are receiving appropriate educational services. However, because academic difficulties, learning disabilities, and related educational problems can contribute to behavioral problems and an increased potential for violence, psychoeducational assessment and planning should be considered a vital part of the threat assessment and management process. Assessment of a student's level of intellectual functioning and academic achievement should be undertaken, with results from psychoeducational testing and assessment used to help determine if a student requires placement in an alternative classroom or other special education program that might improve his or her academic performance and commitment to school. Although school psychological services are not sufficient by themselves to assist in the management of potentially violent students, they are an integral part of the overall process.

Legal Interventions

Although it is desirable for schools to manage incidents involving aggressive behavior among students through disciplinary action or referral for mental health services, the involvement of external law enforcement or court agencies is sometimes necessary. With respect to the individual student who has come to the attention of school officials, legal interventions may range from notification of police that a threat has been made to arrest if the student's behavior constitutes a serious threat or involves criminal behavior (e.g., making a bomb threat).

Other legal interventions available to school officials include the filing of legal petitions in cases where it is believed that a student's behavior is detrimental to his or her education or emotional development. Many states have laws that establish what are called status offenses that permit schools, parents, or other interested parties to file a court petition placing the youth under the jurisdiction of juvenile or family court. These laws carry different names, depending on the jurisdiction, but they are typically referred to as persons in need of supervision (PINS) or child in need of supervision (CHINS) laws. Many behaviors can form the basis for a PINS or CHINS petition, such as excessive truancy, delinquency, failure to obey parental or school authority, and vandalism. In addition, these laws permit the family or juvenile court to outline a series of behavioral requirements to which the student must adhere. These requirements may include prohibiting the youth from associating with certain peers, requiring the student to adhere to a curfew, mandating that the peer attend school and/or counseling, and directing the student to refrain from certain behaviors, such as using drugs or alcohol. Status offenses also permit school officials to file petitions in cases where it is believed that more stringent intervention and controls over a student's behavior are needed. Once the petition is filed and the court assumes jurisdiction, more restrictive interventions may be implemented (e.g., detention, group home, residential treatment) if a student does not adhere to the mandated requirements outlined by the court.

INTERVENTIONS TARGETING THE VICTIM

Behavioral Interventions

Some of the behavioral interventions applied to perpetrators of school threats can also be used with targeted victims. These include behavioral monitoring, in which staff members maintain regular or intermittent visual contact with a potential victim. In addition, regularly scheduled meetings with a guidance counselor, school psychologist, social worker, or school administrator may also be useful in providing a targeted victim with a sense that others are aware of and monitoring the situation. Regular individual contact with a potential victim also provides an opportunity to gather information on the student's adjustment and permits an assessment of any adverse psychological effects in response to being threatened that may require further evaluation or treatment.

It is also important to have regular contact with the potential victim's family and to schedule regular meetings if the situation becomes intractable or if threats toward the victim persist. Involvement of the victim's parents permits the exchange of relevant information, such as the existence of restraining orders that may have been issued by a court, providing parents referral sources in the community (e.g., crime victims assistance agencies), and coordination of information between the school, parents, and outside resources (e.g., private therapists, law enforcement agencies). It is worth repeating that joint meetings between the intended victim and a threatening or potentially violent student should be avoided. The goal is to limit contact between the threatener and targeted victim, thus minimizing the potential for projection of blame onto the victim or exacerbation of revenge motives that the threatener may hold against the victim.

Social and Environmental Interventions

A few of the social and environmental interventions that are directed at the student making or posing a threat can also be used with the victim. For instance, changing course schedules, classrooms, or homeroom assignments, or removing the victim from the proximity of the threatening student may be useful in some cases. Any significant changes or disruption in scheduling or placement should be implemented only after close consultation with the student and his or her family. Although some resistance may be voiced over possible disruptions in the victim's lifestyle, as opposed to the threatening student's, sometimes this approach avoids provoking feelings of revenge in the threatening student. This victim-focused change in schedules is not recommended as a uniform approach, but it constitutes an alternative in select cases where modification or change in the victim's schedule is in the best interests of the victim.

Another means of providing social support to potential victims in school settings is making peers and other members of the social group part of the monitoring that may be needed. Building peer support for the victim is desirable, but it also depends on many factors, including the reliability of the peers who are selected to be protective allies for the potential victim and the ability of peers to refrain from acting in ways that provoke the threatening student or which exacerbate the situation. In addition, caution must be exercised when enlisting peers to provide support to the victim so they do not also become targets of threats or potential victims of violence. It is important to carefully select peers who are reliable and who can be supportive and protective, yet who will not be placed in situations where they are also placed at risk. Mobilizing a victim's peer support group must be done cautiously and only after careful consideration of the risks involved and with full informed consent of the peers and their families.

Psychological Interventions

The decision to refer a targeted victim for psychological services depends largely on the degree of stress a student experiences as a result of a potentially volatile or dangerous situation. In some cases, the victim may not be aware of a potential risk because no direct threat has been made. The victim may feel capable of managing his or her stress level, and a strong social support network may already be in place. Nevertheless, a student who has received a threatening communication or who has been the victim of repeated harassment may be experiencing significant psychological distress. The most common problems are likely to be excessive anxiety, tension, worry, depression, sleeplessness, decline in academic performance, and other behavioral and emotional indicators of stress. If these problems are observed, then a referral for mental health assessment and treatment should be made. The initial screening may occur in the school setting; however, referral to an outside agency or private practitioner should be considered.

Legal Interventions

A major concern in situations where a student has either made or poses a threat is whether the targeted victim is aware of the threat. Research indicates that most school assailants make their plans known to someone else prior to committing a violent act (Verlinden, Hersen, and Thomas, 2000). However, individual victims frequently do not receive direct warnings because assailants direct their violence toward nonspecific victims, or the assailants increase the likelihood of surprise by not warning those who are in a position to intervene. When school officials learn of a threat or a potential threat, a critical issue is whether victims can or should be warned of danger. If no specific victim is identified in a threatening communication (e.g., "I'm going to blow someone away!"), then no specific victim can be warned, even though the threat must be taken seriously and thoroughly evaluated. However, school-wide notification can wreak havoc and may create large-scale panic among students.

Some forms of large-scale victim notification are necessary, given the nature of the threat and the potential violence that can occur, such as when an anonymous bomb threat has been telephoned into the school and requires evacuation of the school building. In some cases, these are specious threats (i.e., false alarms) that disrupt the curriculum and result in lost classroom time. Given the seriousness of such threats, however, they must always be taken seriously and assumed to be real until they are clearly proven to be false.

One legal method that potential victims have for protecting themselves from threatening behavior is the use of a civil order of protection, or restraining order. This involves a student and his or her parents obtaining a court order that directs the threatener to refrain from specific behaviors that are directed toward the victim. For example, an order of protection may specify that the threatening or harassing student cannot come within a specified distance of the victim and must not telephone or make any contact with the victim. Protective orders are somewhat controversial because concerns often arise over whether filing an order of protection will provoke anger in the threatening student, which then leads to violent retaliation (McCann, 2001). In addition, some controversy surrounds the effectiveness of protective orders for eliminating or reducing the unwanted behavior.

Behavioral science research indicates that restraining orders are effective more often than not, although they are not effective in all cases (Meloy et al., 1997). Whether a student should seek an order of protection through legal channels outside of the school is a decision that must be made judiciously by the student and his or her family after consulting with legal and threat assessment professionals who are evaluating the situation and after carefully weighing all options. To facilitate this process, Meloy (1999) recommends that the decision to seek an order of protection should be based on several key questions.

1. What effect has any protection order in the past had on the threatening student's behavior?
2. Has the threatening student engaged in any physical violence toward the victim in the past?
3. What is the extent of the threatening student's preoccupation or obsession with the victim?
4. How well do local law enforcement agencies (and school districts) enforce violations of protective orders, and how well are efforts coordinated between the courts and schools?

Meloy observed that the best predictors that a person will violate an order of protection include failure to obey a prior order, intense preoccupation with the victim, a history of past physical violence toward the victim, and a lack of enforcement of protective orders by local law enforcement officials. Likewise, if the school administration views restraining orders as unwise, shows a lack of interest in the content of such orders, or is unwilling to monitor compliance of the person toward whom the order is directed during school hours, then the chance that the order will be violated is increased. These issues should be considered when making the decision whether a student should obtain an order of protection. School officials should be encouraged to support victims who seek protection orders, become aware of the content of these orders, and enforce compliance with the parameters of the order to the extent possible.

INTERVENTIONS TARGETING THE SITUATION

Behavioral Interventions

In cases of threatening or harassing behavior, an increased risk for violence may immediately follow "dramatic moments," which are defined as events that tend to trigger rage, anger, or revenge motives and that create an increased risk for violence (Meloy, 1997). Some examples of dramatic moments include a student being served with a restraining order or a school administrator confronting the threatening student for the first time and demanding that all contact with the victim cease. These dramatic moments occur in school settings when situational factors trigger an increased risk for violence. If a student who has a pattern of increasingly aggressive and intimidating behavior is suspended for the first time, there may be heightened feelings of narcissistic injury, revenge fantasies, and the like, which increase the potential for violence.

Some dramatic moments are triggered by a personal loss, such as the breakup of a romantic relationship, embarrassment in front of peers, or loss of status or esteem. Other dramatic moments can arise on specific dates or anniversaries that have significance for some students. For example, each year on the anniversary of the shooting at Columbine High School in Littleton, Colorado, many schools around the country increase their security efforts because of fears that students with similar propensities will act violently as a "tribute" to the students who perpetrated the mass shooting. Specific episodes, dates, or events can increase the potential for violence because they constitute dramatic moments in which anger, revenge motives, or the need for notoriety is intensified. Some situational factors that result in an increased potential for violence require behavioral intervention and management. More specifically, increased vigilance and monitoring may be needed, as well as increased security measures.

Social and Environmental Interventions

One of the most important factors that must be addressed in any situation involving a potential threat to other students is access to weapons. The assessment should provide relevant information about weapons that may be either in the student's home or accessible from other sources such as peers or family members. The presence of handguns, hunting rifles, and other firearms in the home of a student who has made or poses a threat to others should be addressed immediately. One method of getting weapons taken from the student's home is to have parents agree to remove the weapons and have them stored in a place outside the home that is secure and inaccessible to the student. It may also be desirable to work cooperatively with law enforcement officers to have properly licensed guns (e.g., hunting rifles) stored outside of the home in a manner that can be monitored by police so that the student does not gain access.

In some cases, family members may be resistant to having weapons placed outside of the home, and rationalizations will be offered that the guns are stored securely and the risk of danger is minimal. In these cases, it is necessary to have parents meet with members of the threat assessment team in which the concerns are outlined and an agreement is reached for having the guns removed at least temporarily until the crisis or volatile situation subsides. However, if resistance continues or parents fail to cooperate, then some conditions may be required in order to face compliance with this critical intervention. For example, the student will be allowed to remain in school only if all guns are removed from the home. A good working relationship between parents of the threatening student and school officials is crucial in gaining cooperation. The message should be given to family members that the intention is to keep the student in school and other members of the school community safe, with as little disruption as possible in the lives of those involved.

The assessment process should also lead to information on other types of weapons that may need to be removed from the home or for which the student should be denied access. One type of weapon that has been the focus in some cases is a favorite knife or collection of knives to which the student is overly attached. In one case, for example, a student who developed acute paranoid thoughts and suspicions of others began to carry a hunting knife with him all the time when he was not in school. As he experienced an increase in stress, he also began reporting thoughts of wanting to kill peers. When the issue of removing the knife from his possession was addressed, he became agitated and more threatening. In negotiating with the student and his parents, an understanding was reached that the knife would not be taken from him permanently, but only temporarily until everyone involved in the case, including school officials, parents, and the student himself, could agree that there was improvement in his functioning as a result of medication and individual psychotherapy. Therefore, all forms of weapons, including guns, knives, martial arts weapons, and clubs, should be removed from the student's home and access to them strictly denied.

Some interventions and practices directed at the school environment include installation of video cameras and monitors, posting of security officers at school entrances, and banning of bookbags to prevent weapons or other dangerous objects from being brought into the school building. Although these strategies are effective for some purposes, they should be viewed as only one strategy in an overall approach to dealing with violent behavior in the schools. These approaches address situational and environmental factors in general, but they are not effective for addressing specific risk-enhancing issues that pertain to a particular student, and they do not help a specific victim who has been targeted or who is being harassed in the school setting.

Another approach that holds promise as a means of increasing the monitoring of potentially violent situations is similar to neighborhood watch programs that have been used to address community violence. In neighborhood watch programs, individual citizens and families increase their visibility in the community and neighborhoods and report any criminal activity to appropriate law enforcement agencies. A similar strategy that can be applied in schools is having students and interested parents serve as volunteers or aids to monitor halls and classrooms in the school.

Psychological Interventions

Although mental health approaches are very useful with individual students who make or pose a threat to others and to identified victims, they have limited use in the management of specific situational factors associated with potential violence. Mental health interventions should be applied separately to identified students and victims. Some of these interventions, while applied to an individual student, can also serve as useful strategies for managing volatile situations. For example, periodic risk assessments on a student who makes or poses a threat of violence can be useful for tracking changes in mental status as stressors or situational factors change. Likewise, treatment of specific psychological disturbances and symptoms can lead to improvements in a student's functioning that bring about changes in the way situational stressors are perceived by the student. In one case, psychotropic medication and individual psychotherapy were used to address a student's acute paranoid thinking, which led to a reduction in anxiety and less hypersensitivity to teasing from peers; this, in turn, led to increased tolerance and resiliency in the student's capacity to cope with negative peer attitudes.

Legal Interventions

The use of law enforcement personnel to manage situations involving potential threats from students can take several forms. Some schools post a police officer at the main entrance where students enter and leave at specific times of the day (e.g., morning, lunch, and dismissal). By increasing the presence of law enforcement, the intention is to deter unauthorized persons from entering school and preventing weapons from being brought onto school grounds. This strategy does not target individual students and is instead directed at the entire school environment. Nevertheless, the presence of police officers in the school, while advantageous in some respects, also has certain disadvantages; it does not facilitate a reduction of students' fears about their safety, and it does not address threatening behavior that occurs within the school building at different times of the day and outside the proximity of the police officer. Moreover, the presence of law enforcement in schools tends to convey a punishment-oriented approach to school safety that is not effective for dealing with the complex psychological factors that contribute to violence. A preventive threat assessment and management approach is better suited for dealing with these complex factors. Nevertheless, certain situations require the involvement of law enforcement officers, such as receipt of bomb threats, commission of a crime on school grounds, and bringing a gun to school.

CRITICAL INCIDENT STRESS MANAGEMENT

The goals of threat assessment and management are to prevent acts of violence before they occur and to minimize adverse psychological consequences to students. However, because a single violent act results from a complex interaction of individual and situational factors, instances occur in which preventive strategies break down and the result is a violent act that has wide-reaching impact. A single episode of violence affects not only the victims, but also other students, their families, and the community at large. An important component of effective case management, yet one that will hopefully never be needed, is a program for dealing with the psychological aftermath of school violence.

One highly systematized approach for dealing with psychological trauma, emotional suffering, social and community disorganization, and other effects of major tragedies is critical incident stress management (Everly, Flannery, and Mitchell, 2000). Critical incident stress management is based on a model of mental health intervention and support that defines critical incidents as "specific, often unexpected, time-limited, events that may involve loss or threat to personal goals or well-being, and may represent a potential turning point in the person's life" (p. 24). Furthermore, critical incidents are based on the notion that the demands created by crisis situations often overwhelm a person's normal capacities for coping and can result in severe disruptions in psychological functioning, such as intense anxiety, depression, symptoms of post-traumatic stress disorder, and diminished feelings of attachment, mastery, and meaning in life.

According to Everly, Flannery, and Mitchell (2000), critical incident stress management is a highly specialized approach that involves several core components for dealing with victims of trauma, disaster, or other profound stressors. As applied in school settings, each of these components has a specific purpose or function. The basic component involves precrisis preparedness that reflects a commitment by the school to training and educating staff for dealing with critical incidents. One example is emergency preparedness planning in which teachers, staff, and administrators learn what their roles are if a critical incident occurs. Also, staff should be trained to deal with the emotional trauma that occurs following a critical incident. Another component of critical incident stress management is large-scale demobilization procedures following mass disasters, in which all components of crisis management are quickly put into place.

Several critical incident stress management procedures are aimed at crisis intervention. One component is individual crisis counseling, which has the goal of returning a victim of disaster to an adaptive level of functioning. Specific individual crisis interventions include listening to the facts of the event as the student perceived them, facilitating social support, empathizing with victims, giving students an opportunity to ventilate and gain perspective, providing symptom relief, and helping to mobilize the victim's ability to complete reality-based tasks (e.g., attending classes, completing assignments).

Several group components also apply to critical incident stress management. These include small group discussions, called defusings, in which the tasks of individual crisis interventions (i.e., reporting of facts, facilitating social support) occur in group settings. The goals of these defusings are to facilitate a return to adaptive functioning, symptom relief, ventilation, and mobilization of adaptive coping mechanisms. In addition, lengthier group discussions, call debriefings, are used to bring about closure after the crisis and to return the person to an adaptive level of functioning.

Other core components of critical incident stress management include family support interventions, where victims' family members receive individual and group crisis interventions, as well as follow-up and referral for more extensive mental health assessment and treatment where it is indicated. A more detailed presentation of critical incident stress management can be found elsewhere (Everly and Mitchell, 1997). However, evidence indicates that the traumatic effects and adverse psychological consequences of critical incidents are effectively addressed by critical incident stress management (Everly, Flannery, and Mitchell, 2000). Therefore, school systems are encouraged to have a program in place that can be mobilized should there be an incident of school-based violence. The individuals responsible for implementing this program should be professionals trained in the assessment and treatment of the psychological effects of traumatic incidents and critical incident stress management procedures. Even in cases where aggression or violence is isolated and does not affect a large number of students, some procedures should be in place for providing crisis intervention and debriefing to students, as well as for making referrals to appropriately trained mental health professionals when the need arises.

CONCLUSION

The effective management of threatening behaviors and potentially violent situations in schools requires a multidisciplinary approach, with input from school administrators, counselors, psychologists, social workers, parents, security officers, and law enforcement officials. It is important to formulate a management plan and to implement strategies based on the unique characteristics of each individual case. Uniform approaches for dealing with student threats or potentially violent situations are of limited use because they often fail to address individual factors that are unique to each case and they offer no flexibility in case management strategies. Therefore, interventions should logically flow from the assessment process. Based on individual, psychological, social/environmental, situational, and attack-related variables that emerge from the assessment process, specific case management strategies and interventions can be targeted at the student making the threat, the potential victim, and the situation. This chapter outlines various strategies that can be used to manage threatening situations in schools. To facilitate formulation of a case management strategy, Appendix A provides a form that can be used to specify variables obtained from the assessment and specific interventions that target each of the variables. This form also allows reporting of an overall level of risk and can be completed periodically by the team to track changes in the level of risk over time. Certain types of threatening or potentially violent behavior, such as bomb threats or sexual harassment, raise other unique challenges. These special situations are the topic of the next chapter.

Chapter 6

Special Situations

Despite variability that exists in the motives, intentions, and clarity with which threats are made, a major goal of threat assessment is to identify those individuals who pose a risk of violence to others, whether or not an overt threat has been made. In school settings, several issues must be addressed when evaluating and managing threats, as the previous chapters have illustrated. However, special situations occur involving either explicit or implicit threats where assessment and management strategies are facilitated by attending to unique issues that these situations present.

Three general types of threats are addressed in this chapter. The first situation involves threats against property, where a student may present a risk for serious fire setting, arson, or bomb-related behavior. A second general situation arises when a student poses a threat of violence against other students, which may include homicide, sex offenses, bullying, and stalking or obsessional harassment. The third set of special situations involves students who threaten teachers. According to recent statistics, the two most common forms of student-perpetrated violence against teachers are physical assault and sex offenses; homicide is a rare but serious threat in some situations that deserves discussion. The general principles of risk assessment presented in earlier chapters are relevant to the special situations discussed in this chapter; however, attending to the unique demands created by these special situations will better inform the threat assessment and management process.

THREATS AGAINST PROPERTY

Arson

According to Sakheim and Osborn (1999), fire setting "represents an unusual or bizarre impulse to set fire and is related to a desire to destroy things by fire" (p. 413). Pathological fire setting is defined in the DSM-IV (American Psychiatric Association, 1994) under pyromania, which is "deliberate and purposeful fire setting on more than one occasion" that is accompanied by "tension or affective arousal before the act," "fascination with, interest in, curiosity about, or attraction to fire and its situational context," and "pleasure, gratification, or relief when setting fires, or when witnessing or participating in their aftermath" (p. 615). Pyromania does not involve fire setting that is done for monetary gain, out of anger, or for some other criminal motive. Although pyromania is a condition that is relevant to arson, it is a rare condition that is found in only a small number of young fire setters (Sakheim and Osborn, 1999).

Fire setting among children and adolescents is considered a dangerous behavior that can result in extensive property damage, severe injury to other people, and loss of life. Considerable research attention has been given to the motivations, characteristics, and psychopathology of children and adolescents who engage in fire setting. Moreover, the general consensus is that intentional and repetitive fire setting is considered to be a marker of persistent aggressive tendencies in young people (Hanson et al., 1994; Rasanen et al., 1995).

The work of Kolko and Kazdin (1991, 1992, 1994) has shown that fire setters differ from non–fire setters in a number of ways, including their relative levels of curiosity about fire, early experiences with fire, negative emotions, involvement in fire-related activities, and exposure to peer and family role models. In a study by Hanson and his colleagues (1994), a history of delinquency did not differentiate fire setting and non–fire setting youth, although a history of playing with matches and past fire setting differentiated a group of juvenile arsonists from a group of non–fire setting controls. These findings were discussed as underscoring the need to take a detailed history of fire-related behaviors (e.g., prior match play, previous fire setting) in young offenders.

In other research on the characteristics of youths who engage in fire setting, Kolko and Kazdin (1991) found that high levels of anger were associated with higher rates of conduct problems (e.g., lying, stealing, defiance of rules) immediately before the setting of a fire and with greater involvement in fire-related activities (e.g., hiding matches, collecting flammable materials). High levels of curiosity about fire were associated with earlier fire-related experiences and greater interest, exposure, and contact with fire. Kolko and Kazdin stated that a combination of both curiosity and anger are associated with greater behavioral disturbances and risk for fire setting, requiring that an assessment of fire-setting risk in young people focus on several possible precipitants. The assessment of fire-setting risk should include questions about the student's interest in fire, prior history of playing with matches, and frequency of fire setting, as well as information about the nature of the fires (e.g., extent of property damage), the student's motives for setting fires, and social context in which the fire was set (Kolko and Kazdin, 1994). To facilitate this assessment process, Appendix D has a number of questions that can be asked to assess a student's risk for fire-setting behavior.

Research on the risk for fire setting has revealed several factors that are worthy of attention. Sakheim and Osborn (1999) developed a regression equation that differentiated severe fire setters from non–fire setters and "minor" fire setters. Nonsevere fire setting was defined as accidental or occasional fire starting by children who were unsupervised or who set a fire out of curiosity. Severe fire setting was defined as "deliberate, planned and persistent" (p. 416). According to their regression equation, Sakheim and Osborn identified seven factors that increased the risk for severe fire setting:

1. Excitement at fires
2. Fantasies of revenge
3. A history of playing with fire
4. Cruelty to animals or other people
5. Poor social judgment
6. Rage at insults
7. Inadequate superego development

In addition, Sakheim and Osborn identified seven factors that decreased the risk or mitigated against severe fire setting:

1. Higher intelligence
2. Severe maternal rejection

3. Sexual conflicts
4. Obsessive-compulsive features
5. Lack of empathy
6. A history of physical aggression
7. Anger at a paternal figure

A survey of these factors reveals somewhat contradictory findings. For example, "inadequate superego development" and "lack of empathy" seem to be similar variables and yet load in opposite directions with respect to risk for severe fire setting. Likewise, some variables such as "lack of empathy" and "history of physical aggression" suggest a poorer outcome, yet they appear to mitigate against severe fire setting. According to Sakheim and Osborn, some variables may change in terms of their relative influence when other variables are either present or absent. That is, while a lack of empathy was found more frequently among severe fire setters, only when other variables such as excitement over fires and revenge fantasies are present might a lack of empathy not constitute a risk-enhancing factor. Instead, lack of empathy might operate as a mitigating factor in severe fire setters who show an excitement for fire and who have strong revenge fantasies.

In addition, Sakheim and Osborn recommended that, in addition to the individual risk factors previously listed, severe fire setting be viewed as a complex phenomenon without a single motive or behavioral profile. They outlined five different forms of severe fire setting that can be differentiated from one another and which are useful for threat assessment and management purposes:

1. *Revenge fire setting*—characterized by individuals who set fires out of spite, as an aggressive act, and usually out of revenge for some insult, slight, or perceived wrong that has been committed.
2. *Sexually motivated adolescent fire setting*—characterized by sexual arousal, pleasure, or excitement as a result of fire setting.
3. *"Cry for help" fire setting*—characterized by a child or adolescent who may have experienced some trauma, such as physical or sexual abuse, or who wishes to be removed from a negative or abusive situation. The fire setting typically represents a desperate, nonverbal signal for someone to intervene. Once the child's needs have been met, the fire setting typically remits.

4. *"Severely disturbed" fire setting*—characterized by psychotic individuals who often have paranoid thoughts or delusions. Command auditory hallucinations may be related to the fire setting.
5. *Pyromania*—characterized by irresistible impulses and urges to set fires. The sequence involves a buildup of tension, followed by fire-setting behavior that results in tension reduction. Although pyromania is associated with a fascination with fire, the condition is considered rare, particularly among children and adolescents.

The management of threats associated with arson or fire setting requires not only adequate fire evacuation procedures in the school, but also accurate assessment of the student who poses a threat of arson. Nonsevere fire setting that is associated with carelessness, curiosity, peer influences, and modeling of older role models may be effectively managed by referring the youth to fire prevention and education programs that are frequently offered through local fire departments. Although fire-setting behavior causes significant alarm due to the potential for serious property damage and personal injury, nonsevere fire setting can typically be managed through a combination of education, family support, and counseling (Sakheim and Osborn, 1999). Severe fire setting creates significant challenges and often requires intensive individual and family psychotherapy for the identified student, as well as behavior modification and regular case management that involves monitoring of the student's behavior. In cases where the student's fire-setting behavior is recurrent and severe, placement in a structured residential treatment center or hospital may be required to provide intensive treatment and to protect the community (Sakheim and Osborn, 1999).

Bomb Threats

According to Dietz (1987), bombing incidents are those "in which an explosive device is unlawfully detonated or an incendiary device is unlawfully ignited, including those in which detonation or ignition occurs prematurely as a device is prepared, transported, or placed" (p. 485). Furthermore, Dietz goes on to state that bomb-related criminal activity includes "the unlawful possession of explosive or incendiary devices, offenses involving hoax devices, and bomb threats" (p. 485). According to data reported by Meloy and McEllistrem

(1998), the frequency of bombing incidents has increased since 1982; academic facilities constitute 4 percent of all bombing targets and are fourth behind residential properties (52 percent), commercial businesses and vehicles (11 percent), and open areas (7 percent).

Although it remains unclear from these data how often elementary and secondary school settings are targeted in actual bombing incidents, a number of false bomb threats have been made to schools following highly publicized school shootings. In fact, Trump (1999) noted that although most bomb threats in school settings are unfounded, in those very few instances where the threat is real, the potential for harm to students, staff, and property is very great. Furthermore, Trump stated that because students see that evacuation of the school building following a bomb threat results in cancellation of classes and that false bomb threats are a means of disrupting school routines or gaining a sense of power and control over others, school officials may question whether evacuation following a bomb threat is warranted. Despite the low base rate of bombing incidents in school settings and the high rate of false bomb threats, evacuation of the school building is a more conservative and sound response to the immediate risks posed by bomb threats. Some school districts may adopt novel approaches to dealing with the issue of whether to evacuate students following receipt of a bomb threat, such as giving parents the choice of whether their children should be evacuated when the school receives a bomb threat. Nevertheless, a uniform approach to bomb threats involving evacuation is recommended to eliminate the risks involved in false negative errors in judgment (i.e., concluding that a bomb threat is false when, in fact, it is real).

If a bomb threat is received by telephone, the person taking the call should try to obtain as much information as possible about the potential threat. Specific questions should be asked of the caller, including the type of explosive device, its location, when the bomb was placed in the school, the time or circumstances under which the device may be detonated, who placed the bomb, and the motives or reasons for the bomb being placed. Of course, the person making the bomb threat may be unwilling (if there is a genuine intent of having the bomb go off) or unable (if the threat is false or a prank) to give this information. Nevertheless, it is important to try and get as much information about the bomb as possible.

Teasenfitz (1999) also recommends that the person receiving a bomb threat by telephone should pay close attention to background noises and the nature of the caller's voice. This information may provide clues to law enforcement officers about the location and origin of the call, as well as the caller's gender and approximate age. Although some schools may not have a standard procedure for recording incoming calls, some means for tape recording calls so they can be played back to threat assessment professionals when analyzing the nature of the bomb threat is useful. In addition, law enforcement authorities should be notified about the bomb threat, and the school building should be evacuated immediately unless there is very clear evidence that the threat is a hoax. Law enforcement officers should be provided with all information that was obtained from the person making the threat.

Given immediate concerns with personal safety in situations where a bomb threat is received, psychological assessment typically occurs only after the imminent risk has passed and the student making the threat has been identified. At this point, the student will likely be referred for an evaluation to determine his or her level of risk for violence. Trump (1999) noted that it is important not to develop stereotypic views of students who make bomb threats as those with chronic disciplinary problems or criminal records. He stated that it is not uncommon to find that students who make such threats have no record of disciplinary problems, above-average grades, and excel in science and computers. In short, the underlying motives, personality dynamics, and thought processes that govern the making of a bomb threat must be examined in each student on a case-by-case basis. A single "bomber" profile does not exist, and attempts to formulate one are unlikely to prove useful.

A student may make a bomb threat for several different reasons. Dietz (1987) noted that individuals who take actual steps to construct and detonate a bomb may do so because of a fascination with violence and incendiary devices, psychopathy, intoxication, responses to life stress, and intense emotional states. With younger individuals, consideration must also be given to peer influences and the possibility that a student engages in bomb-related behavior for narcissistic reasons, such as a need to obtain power and control over others, an intellectual challenge, and out of a need for revenge over insults or slights. Of course, false bomb threats are also a possible means of disrupting school schedules, obtaining a feeling of control over administrators, or as a prank to humor peers.

Meloy and McEllistrem (1998) reviewed the literature on bombing and the psychopathic personality. Their findings suggest that completed acts of bombing or development of a serious bomb-related plan, which are situations involving the greatest risk, may reflect "feelings of anger, thoughts of revenge, fantasies of greed, envious impulses toward destruction, or plans for political terrorism" when psychopathy is also present (p. 559). As noted in Chapter 3, psychopathy can be assessed in younger individuals and is an important variable that should be examined when evaluating the student who has made a bomb threat. A high level of psychopathy should be considered as a risk-enhancing factor indicating a greater likelihood that the student's bomb-related activities pose a serious risk of harm to others.

A detailed risk assessment of the student who has made a bomb threat should also include a general assessment of both risk-enhancing and risk-reducing factors, such as those outlined in Appendix C. However, additional factors should also be evaluated, such as the student's attitudes about bombs, history of bomb-related behavior, and exposure to environmental factors that may increase his or her risk for engaging in serious bomb-related activities; specific factors that should be addressed are outlined in Appendix D.

THREATS AGAINST OTHER STUDENTS

Homicide

Although homicide rates are high among youths age fifteen to nineteen (Verlinden, Hersen, and Thomas, 2000), the number of school-age children (i.e., five to nineteen years) who are murdered at school is very low. According to Kaufman and colleagues (1998), of the 7,357 students who were murdered during the 1992-1993 school year, only sixty-three (<1 percent) were killed at school. Similarly, of the 4,366 suicides that occurred during the same period, thirteen (<1 percent) occurred while the student was at school. Therefore, the data reveal that violent deaths among children and adolescents due to murder or suicide are rare in school settings. However, given the seriousness of this form of violence, significant attention has been given recently to identifying students who pose a risk of homicide in schools.

The very low prevalence of students who commit murder in school settings makes it difficult to predict this form of violence. One reason is that controlled research on school-based homicides is limited by the unavailability of adequate research samples of school homicide perpetrators. Moreover, school homicides occur over a wide geographic range, hampering collection of data on school assailants and limiting research data to that which can be collected from media reports (Verlinden, Hersen, and Thomas, 2000). One effort to overcome these limitations is a research study currently being conducted by the National Threat Assessment Center of the United States Secret Service (Henry, 2000). This study involves interviewing school assailants to identify psychological, social, and offense-related variables that will provide insight into the thought patterns, triggers, and risk-enhancing variables associated with school shootings.

A typical research approach to identifying risk factors for homicide in school settings has been to study similarities in the psychosocial histories of known school assailants. Verlinden, Hersen, and Thomas (2000) have approached the problem in this manner. Similarly, the National School Safety Center has compiled a checklist of characteristics of youths who have caused school-associated violent deaths (see Appendix B). These checklists are potentially useful in the assessment of potential threats of lethal violence in school settings, but they also have considerable risks associated with them.

Although the identification of common factors in school shooting cases can point to issues that need to be addressed in the assessment process, considerable risk exists in using these checklists as "diagnostic tests" to identify students who pose a serious threat of homicide in schools. These checklists have not been validated as risk assessment instruments, and currently no methods or norms exist for standardizing their use. Furthermore, these checklists are often comprised of some factors (e.g., previously brought a weapon to school) that are sensitive to an increased risk for violence, as well as other factors (e.g., history of tantrums; uncontrollable angry outbursts) that are not specific to school homicide perpetrators and which are found among nonviolent youth with psychological difficulties.

The checklist in Appendix B is offered as a means of organizing general risk factors that can be assessed. However, it should not be used as a diagnostic instrument or as a tool for "profiling" potential homicide perpetrators. Rather, the checklist should be used to help organize information, direct attention during the assessment process, and help focus the assessment on relevant behavior that can be targeted for effective intervention and management.

Sex Offenses

Considerable attention has been given in recent years to the problem of sex offenses committed by children and adolescents (Araji, 1997; Hoghughi, Bhate, and Graham, 1997). Although more focus has been given to adolescents who commit these types of offenses, clinical and research data indicate that children under the age of twelve also engage in sexually aggressive behavior. According to research reviewed by Barbaree, Hudson, and Seto (1993), the assault victims of juvenile sex offenders are younger children, with anywhere from 50 to 66 percent of victims below age twelve and 44 percent of victims below age six. Although most victims of juvenile sex offenders are female and either friends or family members, considerable diversity exists in the nature of sex offenses perpetrated by children and adolescents (Knight and Prentky, 1993). The range of juvenile sex offenses includes different kinds of victims, including strangers, family members, adults, younger children, casual acquaintances, and same-age peers. Although a significant portion of offending occurs in the home or community and outside of school, the present section is concerned primarily with potential sexual offenses that may be related to school settings and directed at other students.

According to White and Koss (1993), sexual aggression among students can exist along a continuum, from milder forms of harassment and coercion (e.g., verbal pressure, threats to end a relationship, making false statements or promises to induce sexual intercourse) to more violent offending such as rape. Moreover, the degree of familiarity that exists between the perpetrator and victim influences the relative risk for a violent sexual assault, the behavioral strategy a perpetrator will use to attack the victim, and the likelihood that a completed rape will occur. Many risk factors for violent sexual assault are similar to those that have been identified as risk factors for general violence (see Chapter 3). These include poor socialization in the family, substance abuse, antisocial and psychopathic personality disturbances, and negative peer influences (particularly those in which the peer group endorses violence as a means of resolving conflict).

Several other risk factors associated with the risk for sexual offending are specific to the student's sexual behavior. Among these factors are deviant patterns of sexual arousal, sexual fantasies associated with violence or aggression, a prior history of sex offenses, and distorted notions about sexual behavior. The assessment of the sexually abusive adolescent requires a comprehensive evaluation of the youth's psychosocial history, psychological and academic functioning, clinical symptoms, and personality. In addition, specialized assessment of the adolescent's sexual behavior, attitudes and beliefs about sexuality, and related factors is also required. Graham, Richardson, and Bhate (1997) note that evaluation of the adolescent sexual offender should include an assessment of the following:

1. Patterns of deviant sexual arousal, including evidence of paraphilias, sexual preoccupations, repetitive and deviant masturbatory behavior, and so forth
2. The role of sexual fantasy in the adolescent's functioning, including recurrent fantasies, masturbatory fantasies, and unusual or bizarre sexual fantasies
3. Cognitive distortions, such as justifications for having sex with individuals who are unable to consent (e.g., young children), justifications or rationalizations for using force, the absence of guilt for aggressive sexual offending, and gender stereotypes
4. Capacity for empathy with a victim
5. Attitudes about sexually abusive behavior, including rationalizations, prohibitions, and justifications

Appendix E outlines several questions about sexual knowledge, behavior, and attitudes that can help to guide the assessment process when a student may pose a threat of sexual violence against another student.

The threat of sexual offending by one student toward another is not necessarily confined to adolescents. As Araji (1997) points out, considerable evidence shows that aggressive sexual behavior is committed by children under the age of twelve. Once again, younger children who engage in sexually aggressive behavior typically do so against younger children, and the offending can occur against a family member, friend, or casual acquaintance. It remains unclear how often sexual offenses involving younger children occur in or near the school, or in which the perpetrator and victim attend the same school. Nevertheless, cases involving potential threats of sexual assault among students should not be conceptualized as a problem among adolescents only, as some younger children have been shown to engage in this form of interpersonal violence.

When assessing the potential for sexual aggression among younger children, several developmental considerations must be recognized. According to Araji (1997), specific issues that must be addressed include the following:

1. The type of sexual activity that would normally be expected at a particular age or level of development
2. Whether a power imbalance exists between the children
3. The extent to which sexual contact is coerced through trickery, aggression, or intimidation
4. The extent to which a child's sexual behavior is compulsive or shows a lack of control
5. Whether the kind of secrecy that occurs is expected (e.g., shame over curiosity) or based on a need for control (e.g., intimidation by the perpetrator)

Assessment of sexual aggression among younger children should determine if evidence exists of threats, coercion, aggression, power imbalances (i.e., stronger children abusing a weaker or younger child), verbal intimidation, bribery, or other attempts at capitalizing on another child's vulnerabilities when evaluating the extent to which sexual behavior among younger children is abusive.

The effective management of sexual assaults between students calls for referral of both the perpetrator and victim for more extensive mental health assessment and treatment. Sexually aggressive behavior between students should not be dismissed as "kids being kids," nor should innocuous forms of sexual behavior (e.g., curiosity) be overpathologized as a form of sexual offending. Schools represent a major referral source for children who exhibit sexually aggressive behavior (Araji, 1997), and specialized assessment and treatment services are recommended in these cases. In addition, the family of the perpetrator should be informed of issues that come to the attention of the school, and parents should be very involved in the assessment and treatment process. Likewise, the family of the victim should be involved in sexual assault cases and interviewed to gain information on the victim's functioning at home, as well as to provide input into the treatment referral process.

Bullying

Bullying is a pattern of behavior in which one or more students repeatedly engage in harassing or negative behavior that is intended to control or intimidate another student, who is typically someone in a weaker position (Hazler, 1996; Olweus, 1993). Many different types of behaviors are used to bully another person, including physical or verbal intimidation and control, threats, and social shunning. Evidence shows that bullying is quite prevalent in school settings, with 15 percent of students in Norway reporting experiences with bullying (Olweus, 1993), 25 percent of students in the United Kingdom reporting problems with bullying (Oliver, Hoover, and Hazler, 1994), and between 8 and 10 percent of students in the United States reporting being bullied at school (Kaufman et al., 1998). In a more recent study, Duncan (1999) found that 25 percent of students reported having been bullied at some time during school and 28 percent of students reported engaging in bullying behavior.

The major characteristics of bullying include the repetitive nature of the harassment and the relative power imbalance that exists between the bully and victim. For harassing behavior to be considered bullying, there must be more than one instance of harassment. The victim is usually in a weaker position in terms of physical strength, peer acceptance, or social status. Victims of bullying typically include students who are unable to defend themselves from physical attack, and they often are not accepted or are viewed negatively by peers, making them targets of insults, teasing, and social ostracism.

Some victims of bullying have been noted to be provocative, in that they are both anxious and aggressive in their social behavior (Olweus, 1993). As a result, they provoke attacks from stronger peers and in some cases may themselves engage in bullying against weaker peers.

The management of potential threats of violence in bullying cases presents some challenges because the repetitive nature of the harassing behavior can be difficult to modify or stop. Although the presence of bullying behavior is important to examine when assessing a student's overall level of risk for aggressive or violent behavior, it may also be necessary to examine the potential for harm to others when the bullying involves verbal harassment, teasing, and insults that are not accompanied by physical assault intimidation. Two concerns in bullying cases include the potential for a bullying victim to lash out violently in response to repetitive teasing and the potential for a bully to escalate into more physically aggressive and violent acting out toward others.

Victims of bullying need to be assessed with respect to how they are being affected. According to research cited by Oliver, Hoover, and Hazler (1994), 14 percent of victims experience severe trauma as a result of bullying, including anxiety, depression, sleep difficulties, suicidal ideation, and other signs of emotional distress. In addition, victims of bullying are typically passive and feel vulnerable, leading to feelings of helplessness (Hazler, 1996). Victims of bullying are also prone to develop intense feelings of rage and anger toward the students who bully them, which can lead to fantasies of revenge. These feelings are often controlled by obsessive and rigid defenses that may break down and lead to aggressive or violent outbursts when the victim's coping resources are overwhelmed (McCann, 2001). In fact, bullies with the poorest treatment outcome are those who have been bullied themselves (Kumpulainen et al., 1998; Schwartz et al., 1998).

Based on the effects bullying can have on victims, the potential threats that may arise from bullying victims who have reached their capacity for tolerating harassment and may respond with aggression or violence should be evaluated. Some indicators of increased risk of violence that warrant more intensive assessment and treatment for the bullying victim include the following:

1. In addition to being bullied, the victim bullies other peers.
2. Behavioral and emotional responses to bullying and teasing are odd, incongruent, or inconsistent with expectations (e.g., the victim repeatedly smiles and acts unaffected by particularly harsh or intense teasing).
3. The victim makes direct, vague, or cryptic statements of revenge.
4. Increasing severity of bullying is accompanied by no social supports and expressions of hopelessness or helplessness by the victim.

Perpetrators of bullying are often physically stronger than their peers, and they generally target weaker peers over whom they can exert power and control. Olweus (1993) has noted that bullies often have strong needs for self-aggrandizement and bullying leads to heightened feelings of self-esteem and superiority. These narcissistic needs may lead to more aggressive bullying if the perpetrator encounters resistance from the victim or if the bully perceives that he or she is losing social status and that more aggressive bullying is needed to maintain feelings of superiority over others or regain respect. Some potential indicators of an increased risk of violence that warrant more intensive assessment and treatment for the bullying perpetrator include the following:

1. In addition to bullying others, the perpetrator has been the victim of bullying.
2. A pattern of increasingly more aggressive bullying is needed to maintain status and control.
3. Psychopathic personality characteristics are present.
4. The perpetrator's attitudes endorse violence as a means of obtaining status or maintaining control.

In bullying cases, it is important to focus not only on the perpetrator but also the victim. The potential for serious threats of violence arises not only in the bully who views violence as a valid means of maintaining status and control, but also in the victim who may view violence as the only recourse available to stop chronic bullying by others.

Stalking and Obsessional Harassment

As with bullying, stalking and other forms of obsessional harassment, such as sexual harassment, are based on a course of conduct that involves two or more incidents of harassing or threatening behavior. Legal definitions of stalking generally include the requirement that there be a pattern of threatening or harassing behavior directed toward a specific victim, which creates a reasonable fear in the victim of death or serious bodily injury (McCann, 2001). Meloy (1996) provided an alternative concept, obsessional following, as a clinical and research term for stalking, which he defined as "an abnormal or long-term pattern or threat or harassment directed toward a specific individual," where there is "more than one overt act of unwanted pursuit of the victim that is perceived by the victim as being harassing" (p. 148). Another term related to stalking is "obsessive relational intrusion," which is defined as "repeated and unwanted pursuit and invasion of one's sense of physical or symbolic privacy by another person, either stranger or acquaintance, who desires and/or presumes an intimate relationship" (Cupach and Spitzberg, 1998, pp. 234-235).

The types of behaviors that individuals engage in when they stalk another person vary widely and include the following: spying, repeated telephone calls, threatening or otherwise inappropriate notes or letters, sending bizarre or inappropriate gifts, physical intimidation, and unwanted sexual advances. Although stalking has often been viewed as a behavior that occurs primarily among adults, emerging evidence indicates that stalking occurs in children and adolescents (McCann, 1998b, 2000b, 2001). Moreover, some dynamics of stalking observed among adults (Meloy, 1996, 1998) have also been observed among children and adolescents (McCann, 2000b, 2001). These include the fact that most stalking offenders tend to be male; most victims tend to be female; just over half of young stalking offenders threaten their victims; and about one-fourth to one-third of stalking offenders engage in violence toward the victim.

Although the prevalence of stalking among children and adolescents is not known, sexual harassment is a closely related social problem that appears to be quite prevalent in school settings. According to one large-scale study, four out of five students (81 percent) experience some form of sexual harassment during their school years (American Association of University Women Educational Foundation, 1993). Moreover, 66 percent of girls and 49 percent of boys who reported being sexually harassed have experienced unwanted sexual advances often or occasionally. In addition to the negative psychological impact that school-based harassment can have on victims, recent United States Supreme Court rulings have held that schools receiving funds under Title IX of the Education Amendments of 1972 can be held civilly liable for student-on-student and teacher-on-student sexual harassment when the schools have notice that such harassment is occurring and act with extreme indifference to a complaint (McCann, 2001).

Stalking, sexual harassment, and other forms of obsessional harassment can be managed in school settings in several ways. Some interventions at the school system level include educational training for teachers and staff on how to recognize sexual harassment and how to avoid behaviors that could be construed as sexually harassing. Other strategies include having clear policy statements in student handbooks about the types of behaviors that constitute sexual harassment, stalking, or obsessional following and to identify clear responses by the school system if such behaviors occur, including how students can file a complaint, disciplinary procedures for violations of school policy, and the like (McCann, 2001).

As for assessing the risk for violence in cases involving stalking or obsessional harassment, limited research exists on samples of child and adolescent offenders. Several risk factors have been identified in adult samples of stalking offenders that may generalize to younger offenders. The risk for interpersonal violence in stalking cases is greater when a prior sexually intimate or dating relationship between the perpetrator and victim has existed (Meloy, 1996, 1998); prior orders of protection have been violated; the youth shows risk factors for serious violence (e.g., history of violence, fantasies mixing themes of sex and aggression, a history of sexual offenses); and the youth has strong wishes for revenge (McCann, 2001).

When managing cases involving stalking, sexual harassment, or other forms of obsessional harassment, additional measures can be taken to reduce the potential for violence. As outlined by McCann (2001), these protective measures include the following.

1. Joint meetings between both the perpetrator and victim to try to "work out a peaceful solution" should be avoided.
2. Periodic risk assessments for the perpetrator may be warranted as situational factors change.
3. There may be an increased risk for violence at significant times when the perpetrator has been psychologically injured (e.g., a protective order or a school sanction, such as suspension, has been issued).
4. Involvement of the perpetrator's and the victim's families should be encouraged.
5. The school should support the victim's efforts at self-protection, including efforts to obtain court orders of protection.

6. Interventions with the perpetrator should be directed at assessing for psychopathology, violence potential, and situational factors that may trigger violence.
7. Victims should be provided with information on increasing personal safety (e.g., vary travel routes to and from school, identify staff and peers who can serve as protective allies, develop a contingency plan for transportation if a parent is unable to come).
8. Take all threats directed toward the victim or third parties (who may be viewed as hindering access to the victim) seriously.
9. Try to keep relationships between the victim and his or her family supportive.
10. Make appropriate mental health referrals for the perpetrator and victim.

It is worth emphasizing again that joint meetings between the victim and perpetrator should be avoided when managing cases involving stalking or obsessional harassment in the schools. Although school administrators or guidance counselors may view such meetings as a supportive effort to arrive at a harmonious understanding between the victim and his or her harasser, such meetings rarely result in positive outcomes. Those students who maintain an obsessive or inappropriate fixation on another student will tend to view such meetings merely as an opportunity to be in close physical proximity to the victim. Moreover, the victim is placed in a situation where his or her fear of harm is exacerbated unnecessarily. If the harasser had intended to cease his or her behavior, he or she would have responded to clear statements from the victim or warnings from school officials prior to such meetings. In addition, a risk exists that any anger or rage over disciplinary actions taken against the perpetrator for his or her harassing behavior will be placed on the victim, creating additional motivation to continue the pattern of harassment.

THREATS AGAINST TEACHERS

Although concerns about school violence often focus on victimization of students, research data show that teachers are also victims of violence in the schools. As Kaufman and colleagues (1998) noted, "In addition to the personal toll such violence takes on teachers,

teachers who worry for their safety may have difficulty teaching and may leave the profession altogether" (p. 24). One of the more troubling forms of violence toward teachers is perpetrated by students. Although respect for individuals in positions of authority is a value encouraged by society, a telling sign that aggression and violence are overwhelming school systems occurs when students not only defy but become violent toward teachers and school officials.

Moreover, people have different expectations that can significantly impact how they experience violence in the workplace. According to Barling (1996), "Teachers do not expect to have to manage violent behavior on the job, and they often are given no training in how to do so. Hence, the teacher who is slapped, shoved, pushed, or even threatened by a student might experience workplace violence differently" from someone who is exposed to violence on the job on a more regular basis (p. 38).

Homicide

Kaufman and colleagues (1998) cite data revealing that of the eighty-five school-related homicides that occurred between 1992 and 1994, twenty-two (26 percent) involved individuals other than students. In their study, school-related homicides were defined as those in which the fatal injury occurred while the victim was on the grounds of, traveling to, or at an official event of an elementary or secondary school in the United States. It is not clear from these data how many of the nonstudents were teachers and staff members of the school and how many were visitors or other individuals who were not officially connected with the school. Nevertheless, these data reveal that while most school-associated homicides involve students, an appreciable number of homicides involve teachers and staff.

Given the relatively small number of school-based homicides in the United States, it is difficult to conduct research that might determine if meaningful differences exist among students who target teachers, as opposed to peers, in lethal attacks.

Based on some of what is known about students who perpetrate lethal violence (Verlinden, Hersen, and Thomas, 2000; see Appendix B), one factor that has been identified as a potential trigger is a recent stressor involving a relationship breakup, loss of status, or attack on the student's self-esteem. In students who are prone to violence and who are susceptible to anger or rage in response to loss in status, teachers may be at risk for violent attacks following a critical incident such as being ridiculed in front of classmates, receiving notice of academic failure, having a valued privilege (e.g., athletic team membership) revoked or suspended, or being referred for criminal prosecution or other legal intervention (e.g., status offense petition). Teachers may also become homicide victims as bystanders or innocent third parties who get caught in the midst of a lethal attack directed at another student.

At the end of the 1999-2000 school year, a student in Florida shot and killed his teacher after receiving notice of a failing grade. The timing of the personal loss, in addition to other risk-enhancing factors associated with the case (e.g., access to a gun), created a critical moment in which the student viewed lethal violence as an appropriate means to deal with his loss in status. This case highlights the importance of considering not only general risk factors for violence but also the timing of certain stressors when evaluating the potential for lethal violence by a student that is directed toward a teacher or staff member.

Assault

An appreciable number of elementary and secondary school teachers experience threatened and actual physical assaults from students. According to Kaufman and colleagues (1998), "In the 1993-94 school year, 12 percent of all . . . school teachers (341,000) were threatened with injury by a student from their school, and 4 percent (120,000) were physically attacked by a student" (p. 26). The greatest risk to teachers occurred in schools located in central cities and urban settings; moreover, the risk was greater in public rather than private schools. High school teachers were more likely to be threatened with physical injury, although elementary school teachers were more likely than secondary school teachers to be physically attacked.

These data suggest that certain environmental and situational risk factors elevate the risk for teachers being assaulted by their students. More specifically, the rate of assault is greater in schools located in central cities and urban settings, where higher levels of economic hardship and criminal violence are more likely. Nevertheless, other general risk factors for violence may also be associated with the risk of assault against teachers, even in suburban and rural schools. These general risk factors include a history of previous violence, a pattern of school disciplinary problems, impulsivity, negative peer influences, and an unstable family environment.

Impulsive physical attacks against teachers are difficult to predict and are associated with greater levels of impulsivity in the student as well as situational or environmental triggers that frustrate the student. Other physical attacks may be the result of pent-up frustrations or a wish by the student to intimidate or control a teacher's behavior. These types of attacks are more foreseeable, particularly when the student shows a gradual escalation in aggression directed toward the teacher or engages in boundary probing that is intended to intimidate or control the teacher. In any case, the assessment and management of threats or actual assault directed at teachers should include attending to general risk factors for violence (see Chapters 3 and 4, and Appendix C), situational factors that may trigger a particular student, and the student's motives for engaging in boundary probing (Mohandie, 2000).

Sex Offenses

The victims of juvenile sexual offenders are typically younger children (Barbaree, Hudson, and Seto, 1993), although victimization of same-age or older peers also occurs. Sex offenses involving a young perpetrator and an adult victim are usually perpetrated by adolescents, since sexually aggressive children (i.e., those twelve years of age or under) typically offend against younger children (Araji, 1997). Therefore, in school settings where potential threat of sexual offending against a teacher by a student exists, the case will usually involve a middle- or late-adolescent perpetrator.

One of the most comprehensive data sets on violence in school settings does not differentiate rape and sexual assault from other forms of violence against teachers (Kaufman et al., 1998). Therefore, the prevalence of sexual offenses against teachers that are perpetrated by students is not clear. The types of sex offenses that a student may perpetrate against a teacher are varied and include rape, sexual harassment, unwanted touching, and noncontact offenses such as exhibitionism or obscene telephone calls. According to Barbaree, Hudson, and Seto (1993), when juvenile sex offenders engage in noncontact offenses, they are most likely to target older peers or adults.

Many of the assessment and management issues that were discussed previously with respect to general risk factors for violence and sexual offenses between students also apply to juvenile sexual offenses against teachers. One issue discussed previously that is relevant to the issue of students who may target teachers as victims for sexual attacks is boundary probing. Students may make sexually inappropriate or suggestive comments to teachers as a means of joking or teasing that humors peers. Although this behavior is inappropriate and requires corrective intervention such as verbal reprimand or behavioral discipline, it does not always denote a potential threat of sexual aggression or violence. However, in other cases, boundary probing in the form of suggestive sexual comments, inappropriate gifts or items (e.g., graphic pictures), and obscene telephone calls to teachers constitutes more serious violations of the personal and professional boundaries that exist between teacher and student and requires more extensive assessment and treatment.

Students who exhibit inappropriate boundary probing directed at teachers should be assessed with respect to their general risk for violence, as well as risk factors associated with sexual aggression and violence. The assessment should include such relevant factors as the student's history of previous violence, school discipline problems, family environment, peer relationships, personality functioning, psychiatric status, history of prior sexual offenses, deviant or bizarre sexual practices or fantasies, and motivations for engaging in boundary probing. The material presented in Chapters 3 and 4 will be relevant, as will the materials presented in Appendixes C and E.

CONCLUSION

The effective management of potentially violent situations in schools depends on accurate assessment of those factors that raise the potential for violence, including characteristics of the identified student, victim, and situational factors that precipitate violent behavior. Although risk factors for violence generalize across settings and situations, the assessment of threatening or potentially violent behavior in schools also requires that attention be given to the unique demands and issues that arise in some situations. In this chapter, special consideration is given to threats that students pose against property (i.e., arson, bombing), other students (i.e., homicide, sexual offenses, bullying, stalking, and obsessional harassment), and teachers (i.e., homicide, assault, and sexual offenses). One recurrent theme is that many of the general risk factors for violence, such as a prior history of violent behavior, impulsivity, poor family supports, academic difficulties, and the like, are relevant considerations regardless of the specific threat or type of violence that is of concern.

When these special situations are assessed and managed, it is important to keep in mind another general theme that has been repeated throughout this book. No research evidence supports the notion that a standard or typical "profile" for a particular kind of offender or potentially violent student exists. For instance, no standard profile of the student arsonist, bomber, sex offender, or lethal attacker exists. Like the general process of evaluating a student's potential for violence, assessment and management of these unique situations must focus on behavior, including the motivations and intentions of the student, reasons a specific victim is being targeted, and the situational and environmental factors that may trigger aggressive or violent behavior. Moreover, by focusing on behavior and risk factors that are amenable to treatment and intervention, threatening situations involving students in school settings can hopefully be managed less in a punitive manner and more in a treatment-oriented fashion that has the interests of the victim, perpetrator, student body, and entire school system in mind.

Appendix A

Threat Assessment and Management Planning Form

Name:______________________________ Date:____________

Risk Factors	Type	Intervention
Individual		
Familial		
Social		
Situational		
Attack-Related		

Overall Level of Risk

☐ Low Risk ☐ Modest Risk ☐ Moderate Risk ☐ High Risk ☐ Very High Risk

Appendix B

Checklist of Characteristics of Youth Who Have Caused School-Associated Violent Deaths

The National School Safety Center (NSSC) offers the following checklist derived from tracking school-associated violent deaths in the United States from July 1992 to the present. Follow this link to the *School Associated Violent Deaths Report* <http://www.nssc1.org>. After studying common characteristics of youngsters who have caused such deaths, NSSC has identified the following behaviors, which could indicate a youth's potential for harming him/herself or others.

Accounts of these tragic incidents repeatedly indicate that in most cases, a troubled youth has demonstrated or has talked to others about problems with bullying and feelings of isolation, anger, depression, and frustration. While there is no foolproof system for identifying potentially dangerous students who may harm themselves and/or others, this checklist provides a starting point.

These characteristics should serve to alert school administrators, teachers and support staff to address needs of troubled students through meetings with parents, provision of school counseling, guidance and mentoring services, as well as referrals to appropriate community health/social services and law enforcement personnel. Further, such behavior should also provide an early warning signal that safe school plans and crisis prevention/intervention procedures must be in place to protect the health and safety of all school students and staff members so that schools remain safe havens for learning.

---

1. ____ Has a history of tantrums and uncontrollable angry outbursts.
2. ____ Characteristically resorts to name calling, cursing, or abusive language.
3. ____ Habitually makes violent threats when angry.
4. ____ Has previously brought a weapon to school.
5. ____ Has a background of serious disciplinary problems at school and in the community.
6. ____ Has a background of drug, alcohol, or other substance abuse or dependency.
7. ____ Is on the fringe of his/her peer group with few or no close friends.
8. ____ Is preoccupied with weapons, explosives, or other incendiary devices.
9. ____ Has previously been truant, suspended, or expelled from school.
10. ____ Displays cruelty to animals.
11. ____ Has little or no supervision and support from parents or a caring adult.
12. ____ Has witnessed or been a victim of abuse or neglect in the home.
13. ____ Has been bullied and/or bullies or intimidates peers or younger children.
14. ____ Tends to blame others for difficulties and problems s/he causes her/himself.
15. ____ Consistently prefers television shows, movies, or music expressing violent themes and acts.
16. ____ Prefers reading materials dealing with violent themes, rituals, and abuse.
17. ____ Reflects anger, frustration, and the dark side of life in school essays or writing projects.
18. ____ Is involved with a gang or an antisocial group on the fringe of peer acceptance.
19. ____ Is often depressed and/or has significant mood swings.
20. ____ Has threatened or attempted suicide.

Appendix C

Questions for Evaluating General Risk for Violence

A. History of Violence
   1. Has the student ever assaulted anyone?
   2. Has the student used a weapon against another person? Has the student ever shot, shot at, or assaulted someone with a weapon?
   3. What types of factors have precipitated assaultive or violent episodes in the past?
   4. Is there any parental history of violence?
   5. Under what circumstances has the student become violent in the past?
   6. Does the student have a history of cruelty to animals?

B. Weapons
   1. Does the student live in a home where guns, knives, or other weapons are present?
   2. Does the student know how to obtain access to a gun?
   3. Has the student ever had any training in the use of guns?
   4. What are the attitudes within the home concerning gun ownership and whether children or teenagers should be trained in the use of guns?
   5. How are guns stored in the home? Are they locked or unlocked? Are they loaded or unloaded? Are they stored with or without ammunition? Is the ammunition locked or unlocked?
   6. Does the student have an unusual preoccupation with guns, explosives, or other weapons?
   7. Has the student ever fired a gun?
   8. Does the student read magazines that are devoted to guns?
   9. Does the student hunt?
   10. What are the views of the student's peers or close friends concerning weapons?

C. Violent Fantasies or Impulses
   1. Has the student shown any unusual preoccupation with themes of violence, death, or aggression in his or her writing, reading, or interests?
   2. Does the student fantasize about harming others? What is the content of these thoughts?

3. Has the student ever acted on any violent fantasies or thoughts?
4. Can the student distract himself or herself from violent thoughts?
5. Is there any evidence of delusions or hallucinations that involve themes of violence or aggression?

D. Clinical Syndromes
1. Is there any evidence of attention deficit hyperactivity disorder?
2. Is there any evidence of drug abuse or alcohol abuse? If so, what are the specific substances and their effects on the student?
3. Is there any evidence of delusions? If so, what is the nature of their content?
4. Are there any hallucinations? If so, what type are they (e.g., visual, auditory, tactile, olfactory, kinesthetic), and is there any evidence of command hallucinations?
5. Is there any evidence of paranoid thinking, including feelings of being controlled, that thoughts are being inserted into the student's head, that others are controlling him or her, and other beliefs associated with being influenced by others?
6. Is there any evidence of clinical depression?
7. Is there any evidence of suicidal thinking, rumination, gestures, or history of attempts?
8. Is there any evidence of mania or grandiose thinking?

E. Personality Characteristics
1. What is the student's level of impulsivity? What kinds of problems have occurred due to impulsive behaviors?
2. What is the student's level of anger? How does he or she control anger?
3. Is there any evidence of psychopathic personality traits?
4. Does the student have a history of lying or deception?
5. Is the student socially isolated and/or withdrawn?
6. What is the student's level of social competence?
7. Are paranoid tendencies evident?
8. How does the student defend himself or herself from tension and stress? How effective are these defenses?
9. Is there any evidence of a personality disorder?
10. Is there evidence of grandiosity or inflated self-worth?
11. Is the student prone to tantrums?
12. How does the student tolerate frustration?
13. How does the student respond to authority figures?

F. School History
1. Does the student have any history of learning disabilities or learning difficulties?
2. Has the student ever repeated any grades? If so, for what reasons, and how did the student and his or her family react?

3. Has a school ever taken disciplinary actions against the student? If so, how did the student react to these interventions?
4. What is the student's level of intellectual functioning?
5. Is there any history of harassment, bullying, or other forms of acting out?
6. Has the student ever exhibited any unusual preoccupation or strange interests in other students?
7. Is there any history of suspensions or expulsions?
8. Is there any truancy or delinquent behavior in the school setting?

G. Peer Relationships
1. Does the student associate with other students who endorse violence as a means of dealing with stressors?
2. Has the student ever shown any unusual interests in groups with extremist ideas or radical groups (e.g, skinheads, neo-Nazis)?
3. Is there a history of gang activity or involvement?
4. Does the student blame others for his or her problems?
5. Is the student rejected by peers?
6. Does the student belong to a gang?
7. Is the student on the fringe of social acceptance?
8. Does the student seem to be preoccupied with another peer or adult?
9. Is there a preoccupation with the "dark side" of life (e.g., cults, satanism, serial killers)?

H. Legal History
1. Is there any history of arrests? If so, for what kinds of offenses?
2. Has the student ever done anything for which he or she could have been arrested but never got caught?
3. Is there any history of shoplifting?
4. Has the student ever violated a court order?

I. Family Relationships?
1. How stable is the student's current living arrangement?
2. What is the nature of the relationship between the student and his or her parents?
3. Is there any history of parental criminal behavior?
4. Is there any history of physical, sexual, or emotional abuse in the family?
5. Is there any domestic violence between the student's parents?
6. Is there any history of substance abuse in either parent?
7. Has the family moved frequently? If so, why?
8. Is there a lack of supervision in the household?
9. How do the parents discipline the children?
10. Has there been any abandonment or separations by parents?

Appendix D

Fire Setting and Bombing Risk Assessment Questions

A. Fire- and Bomb-Related Attitudes
   1. Does the student show any unusual curiosity or preoccupation with fires or explosives?
   2. Has the student ever received fire safety training or been exposed to fire prevention programs?
   3. Does the student view fire setting as a way of having fun or playing around with peers?
   4. What would stop the student from setting a fire or detonating an explosive device?
   5. What are the student's beliefs about what would stop others from setting fires or detonating an explosive device?
   6. What are reasons to set a fire or detonate a bomb?
   7. How much does the student know about fires or bombs? Where was the knowledge obtained?
   8. How much confidence does the student have in his or her knowledge about setting fires or detonating explosives?

B. History of Fire- or Bomb-Related Behavior
   1. Does the student have any history of playing with matches, lighters, or other fire setting devices?
   2. Has the student ever set fires before? If so, how many?
   3. Does the student use or has he or she set off fireworks before?
   4. Has the student ever researched how to make a bomb?
   5. Has the student ever downloaded information on fire setting of bomb making from the Internet?
   6. Has the student saved flammable or combustible materials?
   7. Is there any evidence that the student has considered or developed plans for setting a fire or assembling an explosive device?
   8. Where has the student set fires before? If so, why?
   9. Has the student caused damage to property by setting fires or setting off an explosive device?

10. If the student has set fires or detonated explosive devices before, how did he or she feel?
11. How did the student feel after setting a fire?

C. Environmental Risk Factors
   1. Is there any exposure to adults, older siblings, or peers who have engaged in fire setting or bomb-related behavior?
   2. How have parents, siblings, or peers responded if the student has set a fire or detonated an explosive device before?
   3. Do the student's peers have an interest in fires, bombs, or other methods of mass destruction?

Appendix E

Sex Offense Risk Assessment Questions

A. Deviant Fantasies and Interests
   1. Does the student have any sadistic or violent fantasies that are associated with sexual arousal?
   2. Is there any evidence of paraphilic interests or behaviors?
   3. Has the student been exposed to sexually explicit materials? If so, what is the source of these materials?
   4. Does the student show an interest in unusual or bizarre sexual materials?
   5. Is there sexual behavior, such as masturbation, associated with bizarre or unusual sexual interests?
   6. Is there evidence of sexual preoccupation and obsessions?

B. Past History of Sexual Behavior
   1. Has the student ever committed a burglary with a sexual motivation (i.e., voyeurism, fetishism)?
   2. Has the student ever coerced a younger child to engage in sexual behavior?
   3. Is there any history of sexual offenses against others, including adults? If so, how many and what kinds? What degree of planning went into the attacks?
   4. Has the student ever been the victim of a sexual attack?
   5. Is there a history of consensual, age-appropriate sexual activity?
   6. Has the student been exposed to adult sexual activity?

C. Knowledge of Sexuality
   1. Where did the student learn about human sexuality?
   2. What is the nature of the student's relationship with parents when discussing issues related to sex?
   3. What is the student's knowledge about normal psychosexual activity and development?
   4. What is the student's capacity to empathize with others with respect to sexual issues?

References

American Association of University Women Educational Foundation (1993). *Hostile hallways: The AAUW survey on sexual harassment in America's schools.* Washington, DC: Author.

American Psychiatric Association (1994). *Diagnostic and statistical manual of mental disorders,* Fourth edition. Washington, DC: American Psychiatric Association.

Araji, S. K. (1997). *Sexually aggressive children: Coming to understand them.* Thousand Oaks, CA: Sage.

Barbaree, H. E., Hudson, S. M., and Seto, M. C. (1993). Sexual assault in society: The role of the juvenile offender. In H. E. Barbaree, W. L. Marshall, and S. M. Hudson (Eds.), *The juvenile sex offender* (pp. 1-24). New York: Guilford.

Barkley, R. A. (1997). *ADHD and the nature of self-control.* New York: Guilford.

Barkley, R. A. (1998). *Attention-deficit hyperactivity disorder: A handbook for diagnosis and treatment,* Second edition. New York: Guilford.

Barling, J. (1996). The prediction, experience, and consequences of workplace violence. In G. R. VandenBos and E. Q. Bulatao (Eds.), *Violence on the job: Identifying risks and developing solutions* (pp. 29-49). Washington, DC: American Psychological Association.

Borum, R. (1996). Improving the clinical practice of violence risk assessment. *American Psychologist, 51,* 945-956.

Brewer, D. D., Hawkins, J. D., Catalano, R. F., and Neckerman, H. J. (1995). Preventing serious, violent, and chronic juvenile offending: A review of evaluations of selected strategies in childhood, adolescence, and the community. In J. C. Howell, B. Krisbert, J. D. Hawkins, and J. J. Wilson (Eds.), *Serious, violent, and chronic juvenile offenders: A sourcebook* (pp. 61-141). Thousand Oaks, CA: Sage.

Bushman, B. J. and Anderson, C. A. (1998). Methodology in the study of aggression: Integrating experimental and nonexperimental findings. In R. G. Geen and E. Donnerstein (Eds.), *Human aggression: Theories, research, and implications for social policy* (pp. 23-48). San Diego, CA: Academic Press.

Buss, A. H. (1961). *The psychology of aggression.* New York: John Wiley and Sons.

Calhoun, F. S. (1998). *Hunters and howlers: Threats and violence against federal judiciary officials in the United States, 1789-1993.* Arlington, VA: United States Marshals Service.

Cornell, D. G., Warren, J., Hawk, G., and Stafford, E. (1996). Psychopathy in instrumental and reactive violent offenders. *Journal of Consulting and Clinical Psychology, 64,* 783-790.

Cupach, W. R. and Spitzberg, B. H. (1998). Obsessive relational intrusions and stalking. In B. H. Spitzberg and W. R. Cupach (Eds.), *The dark side of close relationships* (pp. 233-263). Mahwah, NJ: Lawrence Erlbaum.

Dawes, R. M. (1989). Experience and validity of clinical judgment: The illusory correlation. *Behavioral Sciences and the Law, 7,* 457-467.

Dawes, R. M., Faust, D., and Meehl, P. E. (1989). Clinical versus actuarial judgment. *Science, 243,* 1668-1674.

de Becker, G. (1997). *The gift of fear: Survival signals that protect us from violence.* Boston, MA: Little, Brown and Company.

Dietz, P. E. (1987). Patterns in human violence. In R. E. Hales and A. J. Frances (Eds.), *Psychiatric update: American Psychiatric Association annual review* (Volume 6) (pp. 465-490). Washington, DC: American Psychiatric Association.

Dietz, P., Matthews, D., Martell, D., Stewart, T., Hrouda, D., and Warren, J. (1991). Threatening and otherwise inappropriate letters to members of the United States Congress. *Journal of Forensic Sciences, 36,* 1445-1468.

Dietz, P., Matthews, D., van Duyne, C., Martell, D., Parry, C., Stewart, T., Warren, J., and Crowder, D. (1991). Threatening and otherwise inappropriate letters to Hollywood celebrities. *Journal of Forensic Sciences, 36,* 185-209.

Duncan, R. D. (1999). Peer and sibling aggression: An investigation of intra- and extra-familial bullying. *Journal of Interpersonal Violence, 14,* 871-886.

Ellickson, P. L. and McGuigan, K. A. (2000). Early predictors of adolescent violence. *American Journal of Public Health, 90,* 566-572.

Everly, G. S., Flannery, R. B., and Mitchell, J. T. (2000). Critical incident stress management (CISM): A review of the literature. *Aggression and Violent Behavior, 5,* 23-40.

Everly, G. S. and Mitchell, J. T. (1997). *Critical incident stress management (CISM): A new era and standard of care in crisis intervention.* Ellicott City, MD: Chevron.

Farrington, D. P. (1989). Early predictors of adolescent aggression and adult violence. *Violence and Victims, 4,* 79-100.

Fein, R. A. and Vossekuil, B. (1998). *Protective intelligence and threat assessment investigations: A guide for state and local law enforcement officials.* Washington, DC: National Institute of Justice.

Fein, R. A. and Vossekuil, B. (1999). Assassination in the United States: An operational study of recent assassins, attackers, and near-lethal approachers. *Journal of Forensic Sciences, 44,* 321-333.

Fein, R. A., Vossekuil, B., and Holden, G. A. (1995). *Threat assessment: An approach to prevent targeted violence.* Washington, DC: National Institute of Justice.

Folger, R. and Baron, R. A. (1996). Violence and hostility at work: A model of reactions to perceived injustice. In G. R. VandenBos and E. Q. Bulatao (Eds.), *Violence on the job: Identifying risks and developing solutions* (pp. 51-85). Washington, DC: American Psychological Association.

Forth, A., Hart, S., and Hare, R. (1990). Assessment of psychopathy in male young offenders. *Psychological Assessment, 2,* 342-344.

Garb, H. N. (1998). *Studying the clinician: Judgment research and psychological assessment.* Washington, DC: American Psychological Association.

Geen, R. G. (1998). Processes and personal variables in affective aggression. In R. G. Geen and E. Donnerstein (Eds.), *Human aggression: Theories, research, and implications for social policy* (pp. 1-21). San Diego, CA: Academic Press.

Graham, F., Richardson, G., and Bhate, S. (1997). Assessment. In M. S. Hoghughi, S. R. Bhate, and F. Graham (Eds.), *Working with sexually abusive adolescents* (pp. 52-91). London: Sage.

Grisso, T. (1998). *Forensic evaluation of juveniles.* Sarasota, FL: Professional Resource Press.

Grove, W. M. and Meehl, P. E. (1996). Comparative efficiency of informal (subjective, impressionistic) and formal (mechanical, algorithmic) prediction procedures: The clinical-statistical controversy. *Psychology, Public Policy, and Law, 2,* 293-323.

Guralnik, D. B. (Ed.) (1970). *Webster's new world dictionary of the American language,* Second college edition. New York: World Publishing.

Hanson, M., Mackay-Soroka, S., Staley, S., and Poulton, L. (1994). Delinquent firesetters: A comparative study of delinquency and firesetting histories. *Canadian Journal of Psychiatry, 39,* 230-232.

Hare, R. (1991). *The psychopathy checklist—Revised manual.* Tonawanda, NY: Multi-Health Systems.

Hare, R. D. and Hart, S. D. (1993). Psychopathy, mental disorder, and crime. In S. Hodgins (Ed.), *Mental disorder and crime* (pp. 104-115). Newbury Park, CA: Sage.

Hawkins, J. D., Herrenkohl, T., Farrington, D. P., Brewer, D., Catalano, R. F., and Harachi, T. W. (1998). A review of predictors of youth violence. In R. Loeber and D. P. Farrington (Eds.), *Serious and violent juvenile offenders: Risk factors and successful interventions* (pp. 106-146). Thousand Oaks, CA: Sage.

Hazler R. J. (1996). *Breaking the cycle of violence: Interventions for bullying and victimization.* Washington, DC: Accelerated Development.

Heilbrun, K. (1997). Prediction versus management models relevant to risk assessment: The importance of legal decision-making context. *Law and Human Behavior, 21,* 347-359.

Heilbrun, K., O'Neill, M. L., Strohman, L. K., Bowman, Q., and Philipson, J. (2000). Expert approaches to communicating violence risk. *Law and Human Behavior, 24,* 137-148.

Henry, T. (2000). Secret service: School shooters defy 'profiling.' *USA Today,* April 7-9, p. 1A.

Hinman, D. L. and Cook, P. E. (2001). A multi-disciplinary team approach to threat assessment. *Journal of Threat Assessment, 1*(1), 17-33.

Hoghughi, M. S., Bhate, S. R., and Graham, F. (Eds.) (1997). *Working with sexually abusive adolescents*. London: Sage.

Huesmann, L. R. (1998). The role of social information processing and cognitive schema in the acquisition and maintenance of habitual aggressive behavior. In R. G. Geen and E. Donnerstein (Eds.), *Human aggression: Theories, research, and implications for social policy* (pp. 73-109). San Diego, CA: Academic Press.

Kaufman, P., Chen, X., Choy, S. P., Chandler, K. A., Chapman, C. D., Rand, M. R., and Ringel, C. (1998). *Indicators of school crime and safety, 1998*. Washington, DC: United States Departments of Education and Justice.

Kindergartners suspended. (2000). *USA Today*, April 7-9, p. A3.

Kingery, P. M., Coggeshall, M. B., and Alford, A. A. (1998). Violence in school: Recent evidence from four national surveys. *Psychology in the Schools, 35*, 247-258.

Kinney, J. A. (1996). The dynamics of threat management. In G. R. VandenBos and E. Q. Bulatao (Eds.), *Violence on the job: Identifying risks and developing solutions* (pp. 299-313). Washington, DC: American Psychological Association.

Knight, R. A. and Prentky, R. A. (1993). Exploring characteristics for classifying juvenile sex offenders. In H. E. Barbaree, W. L. Marshall, and S. M. Hudson (Eds.), *The juvenile sex offender* (pp. 45-83). New York: Guilford.

Kolko, D. J. and Kazdin, A. E. (1991). Motives of childhood firesetters: Firesetting characteristics and psychological correlates. *Journal of Child Psychology and Psychiatry, 32*, 535-550.

Kolko, D. J. and Kazdin, A. E. (1992). The emergence and recurrence of child firesetting: A one-year prospective study. *Journal of Abnormal Child Psychology, 20*, 17-37.

Kolko, D. J. and Kazdin, A. E. (1994). Children's descriptions of their firesetting incidents: Characteristics and relationship to recidivism. *Journal of the American Academy of Child and Adolescent Psychiatry, 33*, 114-122.

Kumpulainen, K., Rasanen, E., Henttonen, I., Almqvist, F., Kresanov, K., Linna, S. L., Moilanen, I., Piha, J., Puura, K., and Tamminen, T. (1998). Bullying and psychiatric symptoms among elementary school-age children. *Child Abuse and Neglect, 22*, 705-717.

Link, B. G. and Stueve, A. (1994). Psychotic symptoms and the violent/illegal behavior of mental patients compared to community controls. In J. Monahan and H. J. Steadman (Eds.), *Violence and mental disorder: Developments in risk assessment* (pp. 137-159). Chicago: University of Chicago Press.

Litwack, T. R. and Schlesinger, L. B. (1999). Dangerousness risk assessments: Research, legal, and clinical considerations. In A. K. Hess and I. B. Weiner (Eds.), *The handbook of forensic psychology*, Second edition. New York: John Wiley and Sons.

Maughan, B. (1993). Childhood precursors of aggressive offending in personality-disordered adults. In S. Hodgins (Ed.), *Mental disorder and crime* (pp. 119-139). Newbury Park, CA: Sage.

McCann, J. T. (1998a). *Malingering and deception in adolescents: Assessing credibility in clinical and forensic settings.* Washington, DC: American Psychological Association.

McCann, J. T. (1998b). Subtypes of stalking/obsessional following in adolescents. *Journal of Adolescence, 21*, 667-675.

McCann, J. T. (2000a). Borderline personality dynamics, fetishism, and burglary in adolescents. *American Journal of Forensic Psychology, 18*(3), 1-11.

McCann, J. T. (2000b). A descriptive study of child and adolescent obsessional followers. *Journal of Forensic Sciences, 45*, 195-199.

McCann, J. T. (2001). *Stalking in children and adolescents: The primitive bond.* Washington, DC: American Psychological Association.

McGee, J. P. and DeBernardo, C. R. (1999). The classroom avenger: A behavioral profile of school-based shootings. *The Forensic Examiner, 8*(5-6), 16-18.

McNeil, D. E. (1994). Hallucinations and violence. In I. Monahan and H. J. Steadman (Eds.), *Violence and mental disorder: Developments in risk assessment* (pp. 183-202). Chicago: University of Chicago Press.

Meloy, J. R. (1988). *The psychopathic mind: Origins, dynamics, and treatment.* Northvale, NJ: Jason Aronson.

Meloy, J. R. (1996). Stalking (obsessional following): A review of some preliminary studies. *Aggressive and Violent Behavior: A Review Journal, 1*, 147-162.

Meloy, J. R. (1997). The clinical risk management of stalking: "Someone is watching over me . . . " *American Journal of Psychotherapy, 51*, 174-184.

Meloy, J. R. (1998). The psychology of stalking. In J. R. Meloy (Ed.), *The psychology of stalking: Clinical and forensic perspectives* (pp. 1-23). San Diego, CA: Academic Press.

Meloy, J. R. (1999). Stalking: An old behavior, a new crime. *Psychiatric Clinics of North America, 22*, 85-99.

Meloy, J. R. (2000). *Violence risk and threat assessment.* San Diego, CA: Specialized Training Services.

Meloy, J. R., Cowett, P. Y., Parker, S. B., Hofland, B., and Friedland, A. (1997). Domestic protection orders and the prediction of subsequent criminality and violence toward protectees. *Psychotherapy, 34*, 447-458.

Meloy, J. R. and McEllistrem, J. E. (1998). Bombing and psychopathy: An integrative review. *Journal of Forensic Sciences, 43*, 556-562.

Miller, M. and Hemenway, D. (1999). The relationship between firearms and suicide: A review of the literature. *Aggressive and Violent Behavior, 4*, 59-75.

Moffitt, T. E. (1987). Parental mental disorder and offspring criminal behavior: An adoption study. *Psychiatry, 50*, 346-360.

Moffitt, T. E. (1993). Adolescence-limited and life-course persistent antisocial behavior: A developmental taxonomy. *Psychological Review, 100*, 674-701.

Mohandie, K. (2000). *School violence threat management: A practical guide for educators, law enforcement, and mental health professionals.* San Diego, CA: Specialized Training Services.

Monahan, J. (1981). *The clinical prediction of violent behavior*. Washington, DC: Government Printing Office (Reprinted 1995 by Jason Aronson, Northvale, NJ).

Monahan, J. (1993). Mental disorder and violence: Another look. In S. Hodgins (Ed.), *Mental disorder and crime* (pp. 287-302). Newbury Park, CA: Sage.

Monahan, J. and Steadman, H. (Eds.) (1994). *Violence and mental disorder: Developments in risk assesment*. Chicago: University of Chicago Press.

Monahan, J. and Steadman, H. (1996). Violent storms and violent people: How meteorology can inform risk communication in mental health law. *American Psychologist, 51*, 931-938.

Mossman, D. (1994). Assessing predictions of violence: Being accurate about accuracy. *Journal of Consulting and Clinical Psychology, 62*, 783-792.

Oliver, R., Hoover, J. H., and Hazler, R. (1994). The perceived roles of bullying in small-town midwestern schools. *Journal of Counseling and Development, 72*, 416-420.

Olweus, D. (1993). *Bullying at school: What we know and what we can do*. Cambridge, MA: Blackwell.

Quinsey, V. L., Harris, G. T., Rice, M. E., and Cormier, C. A. (1998). *Violent offenders: Appraising and managing risk*. Washington, DC: American Psychological Association.

Raine, A. (1993). *The psychopathology of crime*. New York: Academic Press.

Rasanen, P., Hirvenoja, R., Hakko, H., and Vaisanen, E. (1995). A portrait of the juvenile arsonist. *Forensic Science International, 73*, 41-57.

Reddy Pynchon, M. and Borum, R. (1999). Assessing threats of targeted group violence: Contributions from social psychology. *Behavioral Sciences and the Law, 17*, 339-355.

Rice, M. E. (1997). Violent offender research and implications for the criminal justice system. *American Psychologist, 52*, 414-423.

Robins, L. N. (1993). Childhood conduct problems, adult psychopathology, and crime. In S. Hodgins (Ed.), *Mental disorder and crime* (pp. 173-193). Newbury Park, CA: Sage.

Sakheim, G. A. and Osborn, E. (1999). Severe vs. nonsevere firesetters revisited. *Child Welfare, 78*, 411-434.

Schalling, D. (1993). Neurochemical correlates of personality, impulsivity, and disinhibiting suicidality. In S. Hodgins (Ed.), *Mental disorders and crime* (pp. 208-226). Newbury Park, CA: Sage.

Schuster, M. A., Franke, T. M., Bastian, A. M., Sor, S., and Halfon, N. (2000). Firearm storage patterns in U.S. homes with children. *American Journal of Public Health, 90*, 588-594.

Schwartz, D., McFadyen-Ketchum, S. A., Dodge, K. A., Pettit, G. S., and Bates, J. E. (1998). Peer group victimization as a predictor of children's behavior problems at home and in school. *Development and Psychopathology, 10*, 87-99.

Shah, S. A. (1993). Recent research on crime and mental disorder: Some implications for programs and policies. In S. Hodgins (Ed.), *Mental disorder and crime* (pp. 303-316). Newbury Park, CA: Sage.

Silver, J. M. and Yudofsky, S. C. (1991). The overt aggression scale: Overview and guiding principles. *Journal of Neuropsychiatry and Clinical Neurosciences, 3* (Sup.), 22-29.

Smithmyer, C. M., Hubbard, J. A., and Simons, R. F. (2000). Proactive and reactive aggression in delinquent adolescents: Relations to aggression outcome expectancies. *Journal of Clinical Child Psychology, 29,* 86-93.

Steadman, H. J., Mulvey, E., Monahan, J., Robbins, P., Appelbaum, P., Grisso, T., Roth, L., and Silver, E. (1998). Violence by people discharged from acute psychiatric inpatient facilities and by others in the same neighborhoods. *Archives of General Psychiatry, 55,* 393-401.

Steadman, H. J., Silver, E., Monahan, J., Appelbaum, P. S., Robbins, P. C., Mulvey, E. P., Grisso, T., Roth, L. H., and Banks, S. (2000). A classification tree approach to the development of actuarial violence risk assessment tools. *Law and Human Behavior, 24,* 83-100.

Swanson, J. W. (1994). Mental disorder, substance abuse, and community violence: An epidemiological approach. In J. Monahan and H. J. Steadman (Eds.), *Violence and mental disorder: Developments in risk assessment* (pp. 101-136). Chicago: University of Chicago Press.

Task Force on School Violence (1999). *Safer schools for the 21st century: A common sense approach to keep New York's students and schools safe.* Albany, NY: Office of the Lieutenant Governor.

Taylor, P. J., Garety, P., Buchanan, A., Reed, A., Wessely, S., Ray, K., Dunn, G., and Grubin, D. (1994). Delusions and violence. In J. Monahan and H. J. Steadman (Eds.), *Violence and mental disorder: Developments in risk assessment* (pp. 161-182). Chicago: University of Chicago Press.

Teasenfitz, J. (1999). Managing the threat of terrorism in abortion facilities. *Journal of Healthcare Protection Management, 16*(1), 25-30.

Thornberry, T. P. (1998). Membership in youth gangs and involvement in serious and violent offending. In R. Loeber and D. P. Farrington (Eds.), *Serious and violent juvenile offenders: Risk factors and successful interventions* (pp. 147-166). Thousand Oaks, CA: Sage.

Trump, K. S. (1999). How to handle bomb threats and suspicious devices. *School Planning and Management*, February, 1-5.

Verlinden, S., Hersen, M., and Thomas, J. (2000). Risk factors in school shootings. *Clinical Psychology Review, 20,* 3-56.

Virkkunen, M. and Linnoila, M. (1993). Serotonin in personality disorders with habitual violence and impulsivity. In S. Hodgins (Ed.), *Mental disorder and crime* (pp. 227-243). Newbury Park, CA: Sage.

Volavka, J. (1995). *Neurobiology of violence.* Washington, DC: American Psychiatric Association.

White, J. W. and Koss, M. P. (1993). Adolescent sexual aggression within heterosexual relationships: Prevalence, characteristics, and causes. In H. E. Barbaree, W. L. Marshall, and S. M. Hudson (Eds.), *The juvenile sex offender* (pp. 182-202). New York: Guilford.

Index

Page numbers followed by the letter "f" indicate figures; those followed by the letter "t" indicate tables.